Thinking About God

An Introduction to Christian Theology

Fisher Humphreys

Insight Press / New Orleans

Reprinted 1977, Reprinted 1980.

Published by Insight Press, Incorporated, P.O. Box 8369, New Orleans, LA 70182.

Printed by *Braun Press,* Rossmor Bldg., 500 N. Robert St., Suite 534, St. Paul, MN 55101

Grateful acknowledgement is made to the following: Basil Blackwell, for permission to quote from *For Faith and Freedom* by Leonard Hodgson, copyright 1956. Broadman Press, for permission to quote from *The Christian Faith* by Dallas Roark, copyright 1969. Darton, Longman, and Todd, Ltd., for permission to quote from *The Bible and the Training of the Clergy* by Leonard Hodgson, copyright 1968. James Nisbet & Co. Ltd., for permission to quote from *The Doctrine of the Trinity* by Leonard Hodgson, copyright 1943. The Macmillan Company, for permission to quote from *Your God Is Too Small* by J. B. Phillips, copyright 1961. Moody Press, for permission to quote from *Biblical Revelation* by Clark Pinnock, copyright 1971. National Council of Churches of Christ in the United States of America, for permission to quote from the Revised Standard Version Bible, copyright 1946, 1952. Oxford University Press, for permission to quote from the New English Bible, copyright 1960. SCM Press, Ltd., for permission to quote from *Church Order in the New Testament* by Eduard Schweizer, copyright 1961. University of Chicago Press, for permission to quote from *Biblical Religion and the Search for Ultimate Reality* by Paul Tillich, copyright 1955. Westminister Press, for permission to quote from *Atonement and Psychotherapy* by Don S. Browning, copyright 1966; and from *The Christology of the New Testament* by Oscar Cullmann, copyright 1959. William B. Eerdmans Publishing Co., for permission to quote from *Special Revelation and the Word of God* by Bernard Ramm, copyright 1961.

Library of Congress Cataloging in Publication Data

Humphreys, Fisher.
Thinking about God.

Bibliography: p.
1. Theology, Doctrinal--Popular works. I. Title.
BT77.H83 230 74-81556
ISBN 0-914520-00-8

To Caroline

sine qua non

Contents

Contents

1. THEOLOGY

Thinking about God

"Theology" is a word used in so many different ways that it is foolish to argue about how it ought to be used. People are entitled to use it in different ways if they wish.

What I can do is to tell you how I intend to use it. I use it to mean thinking about God. When we are thinking about God, we are doing theology. In this book I am writing down some of my thinking about God.

I want to distinguish this way of understanding theology—as thinking about God—from six other understandings of theology. First, theology is not a study for specialists. You do not have to go to seminary or take classes in theology in order to do theology, though such activities might help you to think more clearly about God. Nor do you have to learn a secret or arcane language in order to do theology. It is true that in theology there have developed some special terms which serve as a kind of shorthand. You can say things more quickly by using them than you can if you do not know them. A few years ago I enrolled in a class in basic accounting at a local university. I did not do this in connection with my own work but simply for fun. My classmates were young people barely half my age. But because they were majoring in business, they were familiar with the terms used in class, while I was not. They knew what balance, entity, debit, credit, subsidiary account, and other words meant, while I had to struggle to learn these terms. So it is in theology. Certain terms have proved to be very useful, although a newcomer to theology may find them difficult to understand. Consider the titles of the chapters of this book. Possibly most of these terms look familiar to you, but they would surely be puzzling to a person who was not a Christian. When special terms are used in this book, I shall attempt to tell you what I intend by them. Usually I shall avoid them unless I feel they are very helpful, since my purpose in this book is not to use unfamiliar terms but to write down my thoughts about God in as untechnical a way as I can.[1]

Second, theology is not useless speculation. We should remember that speculation is not always useless. Sometimes it is very helpful. Suppose you are to meet a friend with whom you plan to ride to school. When he does not show up, you are puzzled. Perhaps you speculate a little, and you wonder if he could have forgotten. That is not likely, since you talked to him last night. You wonder if he could be sick. That is unlikely, since he would have called and told you. Then you wonder if perhaps he overslept. With that in mind you telephone him and find that he did oversleep. Your hypotheses or speculations about his tardiness were useful, not useless. Even though some of them were mistaken, it was helpful to work through them in order to arrive at what proved to be the correct hypothesis. Most of this book will not be speculation. But when I do engage in some speculation, it is because I hope that it will be useful.

Third, theology is not ill-tempered arguments. One mark of an insecure person is that he is hurt whenever anyone disagrees with his ideas. Some arguments about God have been conducted in a belligerent or even unchristian way, and

[1]Technical language may also be confusing, of course. Sometimes it is amusing to try to translate a technical sentence into plain English. Consider this sentence: "This positive regard complex of significant others can become prepotent over the organismic valuing process simply because the infant, to a large extent, is dependent upon significant others for the satisfaction of certain maintenance needs." (Don S. Browning, *Atonement and Psychotherapy*, p. 104). I think that what the author means is that a mother's love may be more important to a child than his likes and dislikes because she feeds him.

that is unfortunate. Phillip Melanchthon, the friend of Martin Luther, said that he would be glad to die so that he could escape the "wrath of the theologians." Many of us can remember vicious arguments between Christians and unbelievers, Catholics and Protestants, Baptists and Methodists, and even Baptists and Baptists. These fights are uniformly unfruitful. But though we refuse to participate in such battles, we must not go to the opposite extreme and cease to care about the issues which lie behind those battles. It is possible to think about God without being angry at others. But it is not possible to think about God well unless we care about him deeply. So while theology is not a dogfight, neither is it a capitulation to indifference and blandness.

Fourth, theology is not a study of theologians and their writings. Nowadays it is popular to offer courses in theology in colleges and universities in which the thought of modern theologians is studied. As a result, many people feel that to be a theologian you must know about Karl Barth, Emil Brunner, Paul Tillich, Rudolf Bultmann, Wolfhart Pannenberg, and so on. It is probably helpful to know about these men, and no doubt our own thinking about God will be enriched by our contact with them. But until we have thought about God for ourselves, we have not begun to do what I am calling theology. Knowing about the theology of others is not a substitute for having a theology of our own.

Fifth, theology is not collating the verses of the Bible. This idea is very popular among many Christians today. They feel that we can set up some general headings like God, Jesus, man, sin, salvation, and so on, search out what the Bible says about each of these topics, and in this way construct our theology. In following this procedure, many feel we will keep our theology biblical. But this is not necessarily so, as a moment of thought will show us. First, where did our headings come from? Someone *thought* them up; perhaps we did, perhaps someone else did. Now this means that we are responsible for them; they are a product of our human thought. They could be misleading. Let me give you an example. I believe that one of the finest theology books ever written by a Southern Baptist is *The Christian Religion in Its Doctrinal Expression* by E. Y. Mullins. But if you look through the book you will find an interesting thing. It does not contain a chapter on the church. I think that this is a major flaw in the book. So even if we try to collate the biblical texts on various subjects, we might leave out a subject with the result that our theology suffers.

Another reason that this procedure does not work is this: we cannot include all the Bible verses. Which verses will you include under your doctrine of God? If you are to say something about God you must *select* the passages you wish to use. Therefore, *you* bear the responsibility for the selections you make. And behind your selection, if it is rational, is some criterion, some standard you are following. That criterion is guiding your theology, so that even if all you do is copy down verses from the Bible you are communicating something other than those verses. This is part of our human subjectivity, and it should not frighten us or worry us. But we must not pretend that we can escape from our subjectivity. To avoid this problem we could just hand out Bibles as the Gideons do. Even then we would have to distribute a certain translation (*Letters for Street Christians* or *The Living Bible?*) to certain people (in hotels and hospitals and so on). So we would be injecting our own subjective choice even into this activity.

Finally, collating the biblical texts would not be a theology because we must do more than ask what the Bible says. We must ask what it means. The Bible is not magic; we do not use it properly just by quoting it. Rather it is God's Word to us, and we must ask what God is saying. When we simply collate biblical texts, we act as if we did not care about their meaning. We must try to put their meaning into our own words. That means we must think about God for ourselves.

Two recent theologians who have written about the Trinity are Karl Barth and Leonard Hodgson. Barth's books are full of biblical texts, and he interprets the Bible at great length.

Hodgson's books rarely refer to the biblical text. Yet in one of his books Hodgson says that Barth's doctrine of the Trinity is in reality an explanation of certain of Barth's presuppositions about revelation and is not biblical at all. I believe that Hodgson is correct. We cannot guarantee that our theology will be true to the *meaning* of the Bible simply by quoting the Bible frequently. What we should do is to think carefully about God for ourselves and then be willing to bear the responsibility for whatever insights we think we have obtained.

Sixth, theology is not a fixed set of truths by which we can measure the views of other men. Many students come to seminary with the idea that someone at some time wrote down everything they need to know about God. Some of them are looking for that book; some even think they know what it is. Once they know what is in it, they are ready to meet the world. They have all the answers, and they can neatly categorize everyone else's views.

What is wrong with this kind of thinking? It isn't just that it often results in judgmental attitudes, though sometimes it does. The real problem is just that it is wrong. No one has all the truth, and no one's views are beyond criticism. Rather we are all growing in our understanding of God. God is out ahead of us, urging us to move beyond the boundaries of any one book or way of thinking, drawing us onward to a fuller understanding of himself. Theology is not finished any more than science is. In fact it is less likely to be finished than science, since its subject matter—God—is infinitely more difficult to understand than is nature, which is the subject matter of science. Theology is a pilgrimage without an end. We may spend our lives thinking about God and never have all the answers. Complete understanding is God's not ours, and any one who regards his own ideas as final has confused himself with God, which is idolatry. We can do theology properly, therefore, only if we are humble about our endeavor.

Now I want to say something about the subject matter of theology. The subject matter of theology is God. In our theology we speak of things other than God, of course, like man or creation or the church, but we always speak about them in relation to God. If we do not, we are not doing theology. It is possible to talk about man in political, medical, economic, or sociological terms. But if we are to speak about man theologically, we must speak of him in relation to God.

In saying that theology is thinking about God, I exclude two other suggestions that some theologians have made. One is that the proper subject of theology is religion; the other is that the subject of theology is revelation.

The view that theology is thinking about religion seems to go back to Friedrich Schleiermacher, the father of liberal Protestant theology. Schleiermacher said that "Christian doctrines are accounts of the Christian religious affections set forth in speech."[1] A Baptist theologian who accepted this position was William Newton Clarke. He wrote: "Religion is the reality of which theology is the study." Since I believe that it is appropriate to study religious life and practices, I shall do so in chapters 8, 9, and 10 of this book. But I do not believe that theology is thinking about religion. Rather it is thinking about God which may sometimes use religion as a medium for understanding God. Our ultimate goal is a better understanding of God; if we can do this by reflecting on religion, we will.

The second idea, that theology is reflection on revelation, is usually considered to be more conservative than the first. Baptist theologian Bernard Ramm wrote that "the theologian does not treat *God in himself*, but *God in his revelation.*"[3] What Dr. Ramm is stressing is that the theological task is possible only if God speaks to us. I agree. We cannot know God unless God reveals himself to us. But I think that Dr. Ramm has confused means and ends. He seems to say that understanding the revelation which God gives is our end.

[1]Friedrich Schleiermacher, *The Christian Faith*, section 15.

[2]W. N. Clarke, *An Outline of Christian Theology*, p. 1.

[3]Bernard Ramm, *Special Revelation and the Word of God*, p. 14.

I think that the revelation is our means. It is indispensable to the goal of understanding God, but it is not an end in itself. Revelation is like a letter from a friend. A letter helps us to understand our friend, but the really important matter is the friend, not the letter. That is why I am convinced that in theology we think about God, not just about religion or revelation.

Nor does it help at all to refine what we mean by "revelation" and then treat it as the subject of theology. For some people revelation is God's mighty historical acts. That is all right, but theology is not just reflection on these acts. It is reflection on the God who has acted in history. Other Christians locate the revelation of God in symbols like "Father" or "Shepherd" or "the cross." Very well, but theology is reflection upon the God of whom these symbols speak, not merely reflection on the symbols themselves. Other Christians locate revelation in the words of the Bible. Fine, but theology is not a study of the words of the Bible. It is reflection upon the God of whom these words speak. We spend too much time arguing about how to use words or symbols. That is wasteful. We must attempt to reflect upon the reality which our words and symbols represent. We must think about God, using his revelation to help us, but we must not treat his revelation as an end in itself.

Theology is thinking about God, not just learning about God. Learning is merely taking in information about a subject; thinking includes an *appreciation* of the importance of the subject. Learning is assimilation; thinking is reflection. Our teachers bear some of the responsibility for our learning, but we ourselves bear all of the responsibility for our thinking. In theology we cannot escape the responsibility for our conclusions. Theology involves us in a deeply personal way. We are not doing theology if we memorize a list of God's attributes in the way we might memorize a list of English romantic poets. A list of the attributes of God may be useful to us in our thinking about God, but we begin to do theology only when we begin to reflect upon the God who is supposed to be described by those attributes.

So theology is more than learning; it is thinking. But it is not the kind of thinking which gives us control over our subject, as when a physicist reflects upon ways to make electricity work for man. Nor is it the kind of thinking which dispels all mystery, as when a detective discovers from reflecting on the clues that the butler committed the crime. It is rather the kind of thinking that helps us understand a friend better. We do not think about our friend in order to control him, for we wish not to control him, but to relate to him personally. Nor do we suppose that we will understand our friend fully, for there are depths in all human personalities that we cannot fathom. But we seek to understand our friend because we love him. And we seek to understand God because we love him. Jesus spoke of loving the Lord your God with all your heart, mind, soul, and strength. Theology is loving God with your mind.

Talking About God

Ordinarily when we think, we use verbal language. That is because such language is the most precise way we have to formulate an idea. It also is the most precise way to communicate an idea to someone else. Words and sentences are not the only ways to handle or communicate ideas, but they are the most efficient ways. I may have an idea without words. For example, I am thinking now of how to get to a shopping center across town. I have learned the way by going there with others. I do not know the names of the streets to take or the distances between turns, but I do know how to get there. My knowledge would be more precise if I could put it into words. I could do that now: Go to the corner where the light is, turn right, go to the five-way intersection, turn right but not sharply, cross the bridge, turn left and follow the curve, and so on. By using a city map I could put names and distances into my description, thus making it even more precise.

It is also possible to communicate ideas in non-verbal ways. Shaking hands means "I'm happy to see you." When a wife kicks her husband's leg under a table, she means "Don't act like a ninny." Looking down at the ground all the time communicates that you are depressed and feel unable to look the world in the face. This kind of communication can be very effective, especially when what is to be communicated is an emotion. But it is not nearly so effective in communicating an idea, as everyone who has played charades knows. So we can see that the most precise way to handle and to communicate ideas is to use verbal language, words and sentences.

Here a problem arises for theology. If theology is thinking about God, mostly with verbal language, does this mean that human language is capable of containing God? Does not God exceed the capacity of all human language to comprehend or explain him? Are not all our words about mundane things, like trees, books, people, jobs, hopes, animals? Surely we cannot contain God in our human words?

It is true that we cannot capture God in our words. The purpose of speaking about God is not to capture him but to point to him. Words are not like boxes into which we put things; they are like arrows we send toward a target. They may not go nearly as far as the target, but they can send us in the right direction. We must remember that even many human experiences cannot be expressed *fully* in language. Can even the best poets tell us what it is like to fall in love? Can the best song writers tell us how a parent feels about his children? Who can capture in words the sadness we feel when a friend dies or the exhilaration we feel when we begin our first important job? Such experiences cannot be captured, but a good writer can use words to point us toward what such an experience is like. Likewise it is possible to use words to point toward what God is like.

All the words we use have first of all a mundane reference. We may call God a Father, or a Rock, or a Shepherd, or Light. But these words, and *all* others we use, are meaningful precisely because we know from our mundane experiences what a father, a rock, a shepherd, and a light are. If we had not had a father or had not learned through listening to other people what a father is, then we would not understand anything at all if we heard someone say "God is our Father." In fact, there are some people whose experiences with their fathers are such that when we say God is our Father, they completely miss our meaning. I wonder what a congenitally blind person understands when he hears that God is light. Most of us can only guess what it means to say that "the Lord is my Shepherd" or "the Lord is my Rock," since we have never been shepherds, and we have little use for rocks (in the sense of fortresses).

So all our speech about God is made up of words which first of all have mundane meanings. Since God is not mundane, all words are being used in a special way when they are about God. How can we describe the special use of words in theology? To put the same question differently, what is special about theological language?

There are three possible ways to answer this question. One way is virtually to deny that theological language is special. It is to speak of God the same way we would speak of a human being. This means that when we say that God is our Father we mean it literally. This way of speaking about God has always been very popular because it seems to fit in with common sense. The problem with it is that it makes God into a man, a big, perfect, heavenly man, but a man nevertheless. Since it does this, it is known as anthropomorphic language (from a Greek word meaning "man"). But God is not a big man, and so if we speak of him as a man we must remind ourselves and our hearers that we are not speaking literally and God is not a man.

A second way to think of the distinctiveness of theological language is to regard it as completely symbolic. When we say God is a father or a shepherd, we are using symbols. Perhaps the symbols stand for our experiences: I feel as secure as if I had a father in heaven. I feel that my life is being guided as if I were a sheep guided by a shepherd. Or perhaps the symbols stand for some reality which is beyond our experiences but which is essentially unknowable. In other words, I do not know what ultimate reality is really like, but I love the symbol in the Christian heritage which says that he is like a father.

The problem with this approach is that it is fundamentally skeptical. It is really an expression of doubt about God. As such, it is out of keeping with the traditional use of religious language in which the man who prayed "Our Father" felt he was addressing Someone. It is incompatible with the idea that God has revealed himself to us, has spoken a Word which dispels at least some of our doubts and enables us to catch a glimpse, however inadequate, of what God is like.

I believe that what is special about theological language is not that it is anthropomorphic or symbolic but that it is analogical. This means that when we talk about God we use analogies. When we say "God is our Father," we mean something like this: "You know what a father is; well, there is Someone who is like that to us. He loves and cares for us and helps us as a father does." When we say that God is light, we mean something like this: "You know the difference between light and darkness; you know that darkness is dangerous and makes you stumble and hurt yourself; you know that light brings security, you can see, you are not confused, and things are clear. Well, God is like light, not like darkness."

Many theologians today refer to analogies as models. They say that father, shepherd, rock, and light are models for speaking about God. I shall be using the words "analogy" and "model" interchangeably in this book.

Theology is thinking about God mostly with language. And theological language uses mundane models to speak of God. Now we can go a step further and notice that the models we use are often qualified in ways that show how special they are. Two of these ways of qualifying models were given names by medieval theologians. They were called the way of negation (*via negationis*) and the way of eminence (*via eminentia*). The way of negation points out the fact that though we may see an analogy between God and a shepherd, God is not exactly like an earthly shepherd. The way of eminence goes on to say that God is better than a shepherd; he is eminently, superlatively what a shepherd is. We can summarize how this works in this way:

1. Way of analogy: God is our Father.
2. Way of negation: But God is not exactly like a human father.
3. Way of eminence: For God's fatherliness is boundless; his love has no end.

Now we must conclude our discussion of analogical language with two observations. One is that even though it is hard to notice it, *all* language about God, if it is precise, is analogical language. Sometimes we say "God loves us," as though his love were exactly like human love. But it is not exactly like human love, which is always mixed up with human needs and with physical and other factors which do not apply to God at all. It is all right to speak most of the time as if our language about God were anthropomorphic, but when we require precision—and in theology we do—then we must be alert to the fact that all our words are mundane models for a supra-mundane reality.

Our other observation is that though we are recognizing, even insisting, that theological language is analogical not literal, we are not implying that it is in any way untrue or not to be taken seriously. A parent whose son says "my head is burning" knows that the boy is using an analogy. If the child has fever, then the analogy is true, and it will be taken seriously. Only a naive parent would refuse to pay attention because he couldn't see flames or smoke issuing from the child's cranium! *The question of truth is just as applicable to analogical as to literal language*. A sentence is true if it reflects things as they are, and it is false if it distorts things. Thus I believe that to say "God is like Hitler" is untrue. Words are arrows which point; some point in the right direction and some in the wrong. Because we care about the truth concerning God, we take the models very seriously indeed. We are careful about what we say, and we pay attention to what others are saying.

Some Characteristics of My Theology

In this book I shall be presenting some of the results of my thinking about God in an effort to help you as you do your own thinking about God. Right now I am going to describe to you how I understand my theology. I do this so that you may see what I am, and am not, trying to do in this book. You may want to ask yourself if you would characterize your theology in this way.

First, and most important, my theology is Christian theology. By this I mean to distinguish it from non-Christian theologies. Buddhists think about God; so do Jews and Muslims. It is a simple matter to see that while I might say some things in agreement with non-Christians (for example, Jews and Muslims agree with Christians that God is transcendent), still there is a fundamental difference between my theology and theirs. That difference is made by my beliefs about Jesus Christ.

For some years there has been uncertainty about what is essential to Christianity. Many theologians have tried to separate the non-essentials from the essentials. Another way to put it is this: what is common to the writers of the New Testament? What do Paul, John, Mark, and James all agree upon?

To my mind the best work that has been done on this subject is found in a little book by an English New Testament scholar, C. H. Dodd, entitled *The Apostolic Preaching and Its Development*. Dr. Dodd examined the New Testament carefully, giving particular attention to the earliest Christian sermons (recorded in the book of Acts) and to the earliest Christian writings (Paul's letters to Thessalonica, Galatia, Rome, and Corinth). He discovered that each of these sermons and letters contained in one form or another a message which Dr. Dodd referred to as *kerygma* ("proclamation"). Dr. Dodd became convinced that this *kerygma* was that strand which ties together the New Testament and which tied together the early church. Perhaps the most direct statement of the *kerygma* is found in I Corinthians 15:1-7, where Paul calls it the Gospel (good news):

> And now, my brothers, I must remind you of the gospel that I preached to you; the gospel which you received, on which you have taken your stand, and which is now bringing you salvation. Do you still hold fast the Gospel as I preached it to you? If not, your conversion was in vain.
>
> First and foremost, I handed on to you the facts which had been imparted to me: that Christ died for our sins, in accordance with the scriptures; that he was buried; that he was raised to life on the third day, according to the scriptures; and that he appeared to Cephas, and afterwards to the Twelve. Then he appeared to over five hundred of our brothers at once, most of whom are still alive, though some have died. Then he appeared to James, and afterwards to all the apostles.

Dr. Dodd's conclusion was that this was the message preached by the early Christian church, that it was repeated over and over, and that it was assumed by early Christians to be the essence of their faith.

We may summarize this message by saying that the Gospel is the good news story that on the three days from the first Good Friday to the first Easter Sunday, in fulfillment of Old Testament promises, Jesus Christ died to save the world, was buried, was raised from the dead by God, and was seen by many of his followers. It is of the essence of the Gospel that it is a story about *historical events.* It follows that theology, to be Christian, must reflect upon those three days in the world's history in an effort to understand God. If this story is the essence of Christian faith, then it must be the essence of Christian theology. This is the fundamental and non-negotiable Christian teaching. A theology which does not take this story, as the early Christians took it, to be God's great reconciling act forfeits any claim to be Christian, no matter how often it may refer to Jesus or to the Bible.

We can understand more precisely what the Gospel is by

contrasting it with some things it is not. The Gospel is not, for example, advice about how to get along in life. It isn't a sort of "Poor Richard" column telling us how to be healthy, wealthy, and wise. It isn't "Dear Abby" explaining how to cope with life in the twentieth century. Nor is the Gospel abstractions or eternal truths. It is true that "God is love," but that is not the Gospel. The Gospel is historical and specific, not eternal and abstract. Nor is the Gospel a new law to replace the Ten Commandments. Jesus did internalize the Law and make it more human (and more demanding), but Jesus' moral teaching is not the Gospel. The Gospel speaks of a Savior, not a Lawgiver. Nor is the Gospel a set of directions about how to respond to God. It is true that if you "believe on the Lord Jesus Christ you will be saved," but that is not the Gospel. Those instructions tell us how to respond to the Gospel. But the Gospel itself does not belong in advice columns in a magazine, or in philosophy books about great ideas, or in law and ethics books about ethical behavior, or in religious tracts about how we are to respond to God, though it may influence what is said in all those writings. The Gospel belongs on the front page of a Jerusalem newspaper published in the Spring of A.D. 33, or near that year. It is a story, a bit of history, a past event, and we must always keep that in our minds when we think about God, or we shall jeopardize the Christian character of our theology.

The fact that the Gospel is a story from history is both a liability and an asset to Christianity. It is a liability because we are somehow offended that the essential thing in our faith is in the past. It occurred in an obscure corner of the Roman Empire. It seems so tiny and tenuous, and yet we are asked to believe that it is ultimately the most significant revelation God has ever given us. That is a trial to our faith, and it hurts our pride too. We may want to ask: "Why did it happen like this?" Surely the wise and thoughtful men of earth do not need to depend upon an execution of a Jewish teacher for a proper understanding of God? Surely men immersed in sophisticated modern life do not have to turn to an unappealing and obscure event out of the past in order to be related to God?

You can know about historical events only in one of two ways. Either you must be present at them or you must depend upon the reports of those who were present. Can it be that we must depend upon ancient documents if we are to know God? Can men in the ancient world, with poor education and limited experience, be our teachers? In short, we find the *particularity* of the Gospel story an offense. We can do nothing to remove this offense, and, if we remain true to the Gospel, we will not try to do so.

However, the historicity of the Gospel is also an asset, for it means that the fundamental revelation of God is accessible to every human being who will listen to the story. Children may not understand abstractions, stubborn men may not follow advice, weak people may be unable to keep rules, but everyone can listen to the story. And if the Christian church will tell this story, all men will be able to hear it and so have a chance to know God.

The historicity of the Gospel is an asset in another way too, because it means that God has done something about the world's problems. The Scottish theologian Donald Baillie has noted that Thomas Carlyle once sorrowfully said: "God does nothing." [1] I believe that one reason men find it difficult to believe in God is that God apparently does nothing about all the troubles we have—sickness, confusion, war, suffering, death. If he does not help us, how can we believe he is a Father? What does it mean to say that God loves us, if he does not do anything to help?

I regard this as the most fundamental difficulty that faith ever faces, and I believe that its solution must be sought in the Christian Gospel that God was in Christ reconciling. We shall deal with this idea at greater length in Chapter Six below, but here it is important to see that the essence of Christianity is an historical event in which God did something about the human problem.

[1] D. M. Baillie, *God Was in Christ*, p. 64, note.

This, then, is what I mean when I say that my theology is Christian: I am thinking about the God who was in Christ reconciling.

The second characteristic of my theology is that it is biblical. Most of what I want to say about the Bible will come in Chapter Two. But here I simply note that the Bible is the witness of the prophets and apostles to the revelation of God which we call Gospel, and as such it is indispensable to our theology. In saying that my theology is biblical, I do not mean that I shall quote and explain many passages of Scriptures, or that I shall try to answer the questions about what Moses or Isaiah or John or Paul thought about various subjects. What I mean is that, as I think about God, I do so as one who has inherited the Christian Bible and who finds it indispensable to his understanding of God. What I think would not be possible apart from the Bible; what I say I could not say if I did not have the Bible. I believe in the God of whom the Bible speaks, and I depend upon what the Bible says for my understanding and my faith. These are not simply reverent words about the Bible; they are statements of fact. We must never be ashamed to follow the footprints of the prophets or to stand on the shoulders of the apostles.

The third characteristic of my theology is that it is systematic. Theology does not have to be systematic. As every youth worker knows, a dialogue with students may often lead to much serious thinking about God, but it is rarely systematic. We can do theology either at random or in an orderly way. As a matter of fact I have found that our best insights often come haphazardly. Even so, there is a place for systematic thinking, and this book is arranged in an orderly way.

The order in which we take up various issues in theology varies from one theologian to another. No arrangement is perfect, and there is a certain arbitrariness in any order. Let me explain a little further why I have used the order I have.

One thing I wanted to do was to talk about God throughout the book. I am disturbed by theology books which deal with the Father, Son, and Holy Spirit, and then go on to talk about man, salvation, and the church. *The Baptist Faith and Message* does this.[1] I dislike this because it seems to imply that we should get God out of the way and then talk about other matters. But I feel that in theology we must always be talking about God. I speak of God directly in chapters 3, 5, 7, and 12, and I try to speak of him in all the other chapters as well.

Many evangelical Christians today have allowed the doctrine of the Trinity to languish. By recent Baptist theologians like E. Y. Mullins (*The Christian Religion in Its Doctrinal Expression*), W. T. Conner (*Revelation and God*) and Dallas Roark (*The Christian Faith*), the doctrine of the Trinity was presented in an uneasy and unconvincing way. Baptist ministers today rarely preach about the Trinity, and Baptist people feel very insecure about the Trinity. So I attempt to give special attention to this important Christian doctrine by saving it for last.

Fourth, my theology is corrigible. It is open to correction. I have tried to think about God as clearly and correctly as I can, but I recognize that I make mistakes. Because we are finite men, we cannot know everything. Because we are sinners, our understanding is always distorted. We attempt to understand as well as we can, but we know that our understanding is not perfect, and so we admit that it must be corrigible. This does not mean that we do not have strong convictions. We do, but one of our convictions is that we may be wrong no matter how strongly we feel about something. There is a certain tentativeness about what we say. We recognize that in the past we have made progress, so we can expect to do so in the future. An English theologian, Leonard Hodgson, summed up the status of theology and the way it should be presented in these words: "This is the way I see it; cannot you see it this way too?"[2] This saying combines strong

[1]This is a statement adopted by the Southern Baptist Convention in 1963. I refer to it frequently in this book because it is a good guide to the beliefs of most of the people in the denomination in which I participate.

[2]Leonard Hodgson, *For Faith and Freedom*, I, 113-114.

conviction with a recognition that we are not infallible.

Finally, my theology is church theology. By this I mean two things. For one thing, I am doing my theology for the Christian community. I believe that it is to the benefit of the church that we continue to think carefully about God. Theology enriches Christian preaching. If a pastor and his people think together about God, the church will grow spiritually. Theology also helps Christians to live a Christian life. As we reflect about God, our ideas about prayer, right and wrong, ministry, faith, and love change. Theology also helps the church with its evangelistic task. The church is called upon to proclaim the Gospel to a world that does not understand what the Gospel is. When we say that God is love, men today think we mean that God is a sentimental weakling. When we say God is holy, they think we mean that God is a cruel tyrant. When we call on men to believe on Christ, they think we mean dress like us, join the church, and quit doing the things that they have fun doing. In brief, the world does not even suspect, let alone comprehend, what we are saying. If in our proclamation of the Gospel we will think together with men about God, if we will do theology with them, then we shall be helping make faith a possibility for them. So thinking about God helps the church to do its work. In this sense my theology is church theology.

One implication of this is that I try to say things that will make sense to most people today, even to those outside church. I am not writing for a special group with technical skills. It is possible to do theology very well for groups with special interests. Theology can be written, for example, for philosophers who live in the thought-world of A. N. Whitehead. This was done many years ago by L. S. Thornton in his book *The Incarnate Lord*, and it is being done today by others. It is also possible to do theology for language philosophers, and this too has been done. Theology can be done for other special disciplines such as psychology or sociology. Peter Berger's book *A Rumor of Angels* contains reflections about God from a sociologist's point of view. There are many "universes of discourse" or "language games" within which men think and understand, and Christian theology can be done within them. Indeed, this must be done if the men who work and think in those disciplines are to understand the Gospel. No one universe of discourse is especially Christian, and that includes the one in which I have elected to work. The Christian faith may be translated into each one. Theologians called this procedure of translation "hermeneutics." They recognize that to do hermeneutics well we must not only be aware of the Christian Gospel but we must be aware also of the men to whom we are trying to explain the Gospel. Preachers as well as theologians must know their message *and* their audience. I have tried to keep in mind throughout this book the persons for whom I am writing. They are the non-specialist persons in the pulpits and pews of churches today together with the persons with whom the church is sharing the Gospel.

My theology is church theology in a second sense; it is done within the church. I recognize that the Christian community has influenced me enormously. I have accepted many things that I have been taught, and I have also rejected some things, but in either case I realize that I am what I am because of the church.

It is not possible to sort out all the influences which bear upon my theology, but I can distinguish some. For one thing I am aware of influences from the great types of modern theology: conservative, liberal, neo-orthodox. Then there are the theologians whose writings have meant much to me: Leonard Hodgson, for example, and E. Y. Mullins, and others. Then there are the specific movements in theology: the ecumenical movement with its stress on the church, the so-called radical theology which raised the question of the credibility of faith in God, the theology of hope which emphasizes the importance of the future. Others could be named.

I am a Baptist, and so I have been very directly influenced by Baptist thought. But Baptists have a varied heritage. Our earliest theologian was John Gill, an eighteenth-century London pastor whose theology was that of John Calvin, except that Gill advocated believers' baptism instead of infant baptism. Baptists today are still indebted to John Calvin for the great teachings about God's transcendence, man's helpless condition, and God's limitless grace. But we have toned down our Calvinism, in part as a result of the revivalism of the Great Awakenings in the 1740's and early 1800's. Baptists grew more than any other group from the direct personal appeals made by itinerant frontier preachers. We have never forgotten the lesson that we learned there, that God blesses the efforts of his people when they take the initiative and go out in evangelism and mission work to lead men to have a conversion experience with Christ. Most Baptists today cannot even visualize a non-evangelistic and non-mission church. So our initial Calvinism was modified by revivalism and missions.

In the 1850's there grew up among Southern Baptists a group called Landmark Baptists. They had a different view of the church than earlier Baptists had. They felt that since Baptists were the only ones who baptized believers, Baptist churches were the only true churches. This very exclusive view led to many controversies and has had great influence upon all Southern Baptists. Even today, more than a hundred years later, many Baptists believe that this is the only true Baptist position. While I reject Landmark exclusivism, one thing which they taught is important in my theology. I believe that a local congregation of Christians has a special place in God's work. I shall be explaining what I mean by this in Chapter Ten.

In the 1900's a movement grew up in America called Fundamentalism. It was named for some books which were published about 1910-15. The movement had followers in most denominations including Baptists; in this sense it was ecumenical. It was in part a reaction to liberal Protestant views which were then widespread and which have been vigorously summarized by H. Richard Niebuhr in a famous sentence:

> A God without wrath brought men without sin into a kingdom without judgment through the ministrations of a Christ without a cross.[1]

In the face of this view the Fundamentalists asserted what they felt were fundamental teachings of Christian faith. Generally speaking I believe that it was good for the church to be recalled to fundamental Christian teachings. What I regret about Fundamentalism, apart from its hostility and its narrow mindedness, is its failure to define what I believe to be the *really* fundamental issues of faith. I regard God as the most fundamental issue of all. In *The Fundamentals* what was said about God was not very helpful, and in any case it was lost sight of in the midst of debates about non-fundamental matters about the authorship of Genesis or Isaiah. Further, I believe that the central Christian teaching is the Gospel. That fundamental is also obscured in *The Fundamentals*. Settling on what is fundamental is something each of us must do for himself.

Ironically, among Baptists Fundamentalism opened the door for new teachings to come in. For example, Baptists seem to have accepted dispensationalism at this time. Dispensationalism is a method of interpreting the Bible which divides history into several periods (dispensations) during which God dealt with men in different ways. The Scofield Reference Bible popularized dispensationalism among Baptists, and today many Baptists find it hard to understand that dispensationalism, and especially its view of the end of the world (eschatology), has not always been part of the Baptist heritage.

The point of my sketching part of the Baptist heritage is to make clear that we never think about God in a vacuum. We all have a heritage. If we are aware of our heritage, then it will help us; if we do not recognize that our heritage

[1]H. Richard Niebuhr, *The Kingdom of God in America*, p. 193.

influences us, then it will enslave us.

In summary, theology is thinking about God. In doing theology we use words which are earthly models for spiritual realities. My theology is Christian because it is about God in Christ reconciling. It is biblical, systematic, and corrigible. And it is influenced by the rich Christian heritage and especially by the Baptist heritage.

For further reading:

My conviction that theology is thinking about God is similar to the view of A. H. Strong in his *Systematic Theology*, I, 1-51. Unfortunately Strong's presentation is so formal that it is lifeless. The best theological discussion of analogy that I know of is that of G. F. Woods in *Theological Explanation.* A more current presentation, in terms of models and qualifiers, is made by Ian T. Ramsey in *Religious Language*. For the meaning of Gospel see C. H. Dodd, *The Apostolic Preaching and Its Development.* I have found Leonard Hodgson's first volume of *For Faith and Freedom*, chapters 1-5, very helpful in trying to state the conviction theologians have that their ideas are both true and corrigible. In *A Rumor of Angels* Peter Berger shows how theology can be both relative and true. For a readable and delightful presentation of the Baptist theological heritage see Walter B. Shurden, *Not a Silent People.* For a view of the wider Protestant heritage the book *Protestant Theology* by John Dillenberger and Claude Welch is a classic.

2. REVELATION

Introduction

As Christians we believe that God speaks to men about himself. That is what we mean when we say that God reveals himself. Whatever God says to us is a revelation of God.

The purpose of God's revelation is that men come to know him. This means both to know facts about God and to know God through having a personal relationship with him.[1]

When God speaks to us, it is an act of grace. He is God and we are only men; to be addressed by God is a privilege for us. It is especially gracious for God to reveal himself so that our knowledge of him may go on to become a personal relationship with him.

Revelation is indispensable if we are to know God personally. We all recognize that in our relationships with other people we can really know another person only if he reveals himself to us. We may observe his appearance, life style, or history on our own. But if we are to know him personally—his fears, dreams, needs, ideas, feelings—he must tell us about himself. Similarly we can know God personally only if he speaks to us.

[1]Karl Barth, a Swiss theologian who died in 1968, is responsible for revelation having the prominence it does in modern theology. Barth used the word "revelation" in the narrower sense of God's establishing a personal relationship with man. This is a fair thing to do. I have chosen to use the word in a wider sense because I want to stress that all knowledge of God comes by revelation, even if that knowledge is scanty. I fully agree with Barth's view that the ideal revelation of God is a personal relationship.

When we say that God speaks, we are using an analogy from human life. We are saying something like this: "You know what it is to be with a friend, to watch him act, and to listen to him explain what he's doing, letting you share in his life. Well, God has done something like that for us. He has let us be with him, watching him act. He has opened his heart and explained to us what he is doing." That is what it means to say that God is revealing himself to us.

One of the most vexed questions for theologians is how God speaks to us. We know how other people speak to us. They use gestures and facial expressions. They say words and sentences. These sounds, gestures, and expressions are the media through which they communicate to us. Since God does not have a body (that is usually what we mean when we say that God is Spirit; see John 4:19-24), he does not speak to us through these media. What media does he use?

There are two things I want to say about the media of God's revelation. One is that God is free to use any medium he chooses. I am not in a position to say that God can speak only in this way and not in that way, nor is anyone else. God is free; we cannot confine his revelation to media that suit us.

Also, as Christians we are convinced that the ultimate medium of God's revelation is Jesus Christ. Because he is such a special Word of God (see John 1:1-14), I shall be speaking about him in separate chapters later on.

Medium One: Nature

In Chapter Three we will discuss what it means to say that God created the world. For the moment we shall assume that he did create the world; and we observe that if the world was made by God then it very well may say something to us about God.

I believe that it does. In Romans, Paul observes that God's power and deity have been made visible to men's reason by the world which God made (Romans 1:19-20). In Psalms it is said that the heavens declare God's glory (Psalm 19:1). Men who have never read these passages from the Bible have come to recognize God's power and glory through their observation of nature. I remember once standing on a balcony with a friend and watching a sunset. My friend said: "How can anyone see something that beautiful and not believe in God?" Through the sunset God was revealing himself to my friend.

When a man makes something, he tells us something about himself. If he designs a building, writes a novel, builds a racing car, or plans a factory, he says something about himself. If his work is done well, we learn that he is efficient or clever or has good taste. It is in this sense that God reveals himself through nature.

But not everything a man makes is equally revelatory of him. A letter he writes will be more revealing than a table he builds. So not all of nature is equally revelatory of God. Much of it is ambiguous. Mark Twain once made a joke about mosquitoes—why would God create such a thing as a mosquito? I do not think that Mark Twain was entirely correct, but I see his point. Also, some things in nature seem to speak against God. Natural disasters like floods or earthquakes cause great suffering. Instead of helping us to understand God, they seem to contradict what we have learned about God through other media.

Also, people have different attitudes toward nature. Some regard it simply as a given fact and do not expect it to point to anything beyond itself. Nature is to be used for man's convenience, nothing more. Other people have more of a sense of awe before nature. They look to it to point beyond itself. They expect it to convey messages. It is people who have this sense of wonder about our world to whom God speaks through nature.

In summary, the revelation God gives through nature is partial and ambiguous. For a personal knowledge of God we need more than what God says to us through nature. We must go on now to consider other media of God's self-revelation.

Medium Two: History

The word "history" may mean either events in men's lives or the story of those events as written or told by an historian. I believe that God acts in men's lives in a way that helps us to see what God is like. Moreover, I believe that as the story of those activities is told God speaks to those who are listening.

History is very different from nature. Nature moves in cycles, but history moves on a straight line. Nature repeats itself: one rose is very much like another. History does not repeat itself: each man is unique, each event is unrepeatable.

Theologians have distinguished these two media of revelation by calling the revelation through nature "general revelation" and the one through history "special revelation." To be more specific, in nature we see God's creative activity, while in history we see God's saving activity. Naturally the second revelation is more important to us; it opens up to us the possibility of having a personal relationship with God.

Two questions arise about God's revelation through history. The first is: Which events of history reveal God? The second is: How does God act in history?

Certainly not all events of history are equally revelatory of God. What does the barbaric cruelty of the wars of the twentieth century reveal about God? What does the settling of the American West say to us about God? These say nothing as far as I can tell.

In Chapter One I pointed out that Christians believe that in a particular portion of the world's history, the story of the Jewish people climaxed by the life of Jesus and his sacrifice, God acted in a redemptive way. I believe that, as unlikely as it seems, this small segment of history is the ultimate revelation we have of God. Surely that is what the Jews and early Christians believed.

The religion of Israel was founded upon God's great Exodus deliverance of the people from Egypt. This stands in sharp contrast to the religions of Israel's neighbors which were founded solely upon nature. The Israelite preoccupation with history is summed up in this passage from Deuteronomy:

> You are a people holy to the Lord your God; the Lord your God chose you out of all nations on earth to be his special possession. It was not because you were more numerous than any other nation that the Lord cared for you and chose you, for you were the smallest of all nations; it was because the Lord loved you and stood by his oath to your forefathers, that he brought you out with his strong hand and redeemed you from the land of slavery, from the power of Pharaoh King of Egypt. (Deuteronomy 7:6-8)

Israelite religion was a conviction that God had acted in history to save Israel. Jewish ceremonies, laws, prayers, and songs presupposed that when Israel came from Egypt to become a nation and to settle in Palestine, it was by God's action. Israelite theology consisted fundamentally of reciting the mighty acts which God had done for his people.

In the New Testament, Christians have the same attitude about Jesus and his sacrifice that the Israelites had about the Exodus. In fact, Jesus' sacrifice is referred to in the New Testament as "his exodus" (Luke 9:30-31). We shall be looking into the revelation given in Jesus more fully in chapters five and six.

Right now the point is that certain things have occurred in history through which God has spoken to us. While God has perhaps spoken through many events of history, as Christians we find his clearest revelation in the history of Israel and especially in that part of it which is the life of Jesus.

The other question about history is: How does God act in it to render it a medium of revelation?

It is always difficult to answer "how" questions about God, and it is not hard to see why. When you ask a "how" question about a man, you respond in terms of his physical body. How does he walk?—on his feet. How does he speak?—with his mouth. How does he write?—with his hands. But God does not have a body, so it is difficult to answer a "how" question about him. What this question really means is: What is the identifying mark of an act of God? How can I spot an event in history through which God is speaking?

Many Christians feel that God's acts are all characterized by miracles. I believe that God has from time to time done miracles, some of which are recorded in the Bible, but I do not believe that they are an essential aspect of God's revelatory acts in history. An event in history may be an act of God without being miraculous. When Jesus preached his sermons, God was acting to reveal himself just as much as when Jesus healed the sick.

If not miracles, then what is the identifying mark of an act of God in history? The answer, I think, is that there is not an identifying mark. The only difference between a revelatory act and a non-revelatory one is that God reveals himself through one and not through the other.

Then how do we identify the revelatory acts? I believe that we depend upon men who are gifted with insight into such matters to tell us that God was speaking. Moses told Israel that God was at work in the Exodus; Isaiah told Israel that God was speaking in Israel's military defeats; the apostles told the church that God was in Christ reconciling. We are thus dependent upon these witnesses to the acts of God to identify God for us in the events. We may not like this dependence but it nevertheless exists, and we must acknowledge it.

We noted in Chapter One that there are only two ways to know about an historical event; either we must be present when it happened or we must depend upon the testimony of someone who was present. For the revelatory acts of God in Israel's history we depend upon the witness of the Bible. But the writers of The Bible gave us more than a bare record of what they saw; they interpreted what they saw as the activity of God. The early Christians did not say only that Christ died; they said that he died "for our sins according to the Scriptures." So the apostles and prophets give us an interpretation of the meaning of what they saw.

Two questions arise concerning their interpretation. Is it

true? And if they have interpreted things, does this mean that we today must cease attempting to interpret and must be satisfied to accept uncritically what they said? We shall answer the first question when we come to speak more directly about the Bible.

I am convinced that the fact that the apostles interpreted the meaning of the revelatory history which they witnessed does not mean at all that we must accept it uncritically. We depend on them to tell us that something occurred (for example, Christ died and was resurrected). We depend on them to call our attention to the fact that God was at work in these events (for example, God was in Christ reconciling). But we must still reflect *just as seriously as they did* upon these events and how they are to be understood. Thoughtless repetition of the witness of the apostles is not a faithful response to the thoughtful witness of the apostles. To be a good student of Paul or John is not to ask Paul or John to do your thinking for you. A good student of the apostles will look at the events through their eyes and think along with them about how to understand what they witnessed.

Medium Three: The Bible

God speaks to us through the Bible. We have already said that the Bible is an indispensable witness to the acts of God in history, especially to the Gospel events. We have acknowledged our dependence upon the prophetic and apostolic interpretation of the acts of God. And we have affirmed that this dependence is compatible with a consciously critical reading of the Bible.

Two questions remain to be asked about the Bible. The first is the more controversial: What shall we say about the Bible? The second is the more important: What shall we do with the Bible? We shall deal first with the more controversial question.

The Baptist Faith and Message says that the Bible "is, and will remain to the end of the world, the true center of Christian union." I wish this were true, but to me it seems like wishful thinking. Among Southern Baptists, at least, the Bible is our most divisive issue, not the center of union. People who can agree on many other issues in the Christian faith cannot agree on what to say about the Bible. It is widely believed that this issue is the most fundamental one of all.

One of the ways in which the Bible has been discussed is in terms of its inspiration. There have been debates about whether the Bible was inspired by dictation (God spoke the words and ignored the writers' minds), by plenary verbal method (God inspired the words but worked through the writers' minds), or dynamically (God inspired the ideas but not the words). This debate cannot be resolved for a simple reason: we do not have any data for resolving it. The concept of inspiration, which means breathing-in, appears only once in the Bible, in an ambigious passage (II Timothy 3:16). Inspiration is therefore a minor biblical idea in contrast, for example, to the concept of the Word of God which occurs literally thousands of times in the Bible. Therefore it is my judgment that we should discuss the Bible in terms other than inspiration. Like *The Baptist Faith and Message*, I affirm the inspiration of the Bible as a fact, but I do not try to define it.

A second way in which the Bible is discussed is in terms of its authority. Authority is a complex issue, but what we usually mean by it is simply the right to be followed or accepted. When we speak generally of belief, it is fairly simple to say what we must believe: we must believe the truth. So the authority of the Bible is the right of the Bible to be believed because it tells us the truth. Therefore authority means truth, and it is in terms of truth that we shall speak of the Bible.

There is much agreement among Christians about the truth of the Bible. Since the Gospel comes to us through the Bible, and since Christians are people who believe that the Gospel is true, clearly we have a large measure of agreement. And, let us notice, this agreement concerns the most central Christian message, that God was in Christ reconciling.

If this is true—and to me it seems inescapable—then we must acknowledge that the issues which divide Christians are in a real sense secondary ones. If the fact that God was in Christ reconciling is the fundamental Christian fact, then others are secondary. The only alternative is to say that the Gospel is not the fundamental Christian fact. I find it difficult to believe that any Christian could say this. Who would preach another Gospel? Who would elevate any other aspect even of Christian faith to the eminence that belongs to the Gospel alone? Who would insist that we must go beyond this Gospel in our quests for unity and for maturity? To attempt to find anything more profound than that God was in Christ reconciling is to settle for something inferior and possibly false.

So I take it that *all Christians agree about the Gospel.* They disagree only about matters in Scripture which are secondary to the Gospel. But on the central issue they agree.

Now let us consider the vexed question: What shall we say about the biblical records of dates, names, places, numbers of people, and all the other thousands of facts which are mentioned in the Bible?

It is here that Christians divide into two groups. One group says that every fact recorded in the Bible is accurate; the Bible is inerrant. The other group says that the Bible contains facts which are not accurate; it is errant. Which position is the correct one?

On the surface no two positions could be more fully opposed than these two seem to be. Even so, I have come to believe that the two positions are not really opposites. I believe that, in fact, they can be reconciled, and I believe that if you will consider the evidence that I give for it you will understand why I hold this position. I hope that you will agree with me; but even if you do not, perhaps you can see the point I am trying to make.

Before I give my evidence, let me say something about the reasons that these two positions, inerrancy and errancy, are held. These positions are based upon different kinds of logic.

The position that the Bible is inerrant is based upon deductive logic. Deductive arguments traditionally have a major and minor premise and can be put into a form called a syllogism. Here are two syllogisms which support inerrancy.

> The Bible is God's Word.
> God is truthful.
> *The Bible is truthful.*
>
> Jesus accepted the Bible as truthful.
> Jesus was divine and truthful.
> *The Bible is truthful.*

Both these syllogisms seem to me to have correct premises and to be in proper form, so their conclusions are true.

In addition to these deductive arguments, inerrancy receives support from other less formal arguments. For example: If the Bible contains even one error, it cannot be trusted at all. This is the "domino" argument: If one domino falls, they all fall down. I do not believe that this argument is true.

Another argument is: If we Christians would all agree about the Bible, we could solve all our other problems. This argument fails to take account of the fact that we Christians are still sinners. In the past all Christians agreed that the Bible was inerrant, but they did not get along with each other well. In the eighteenth century Lutherans, Baptists, Catholics, and Quakers agreed that the Bible was inerrant, but since they interpreted it differently, they did not get along well nor did they solve all their problems.

Another argument used to support inerrancy is that the Bible is the foundation upon which our faith rests, and unless the foundation is solid, or straight, everything else will be endangered, or crooked. This is similar to the domino theory, but more persuasive, because it makes you wonder if you dare take any other position than inerrancy. Isn't it somehow disloyal to jeopardize everything in the Christian faith by denying inerrancy? I have already disagreed with this argument by asserting that the fundamental issue is not what we say about the Bible, but it is the Gospel. And I shall disagree with it below for another reason.

My conclusion here is that the really firm support for inerrancy comes from the deductive arguments. Now let us see what kind of evidence supports the errancy position.

The answer is that the evidence in favor of errancy is not deductive; it is inductive. This means that as people read the Bible they see things that seem to them to be inaccurate. From this they draw a general conclusion that the Bible is errant.

Let us illustrate the kind of evidence that leads to this conclusion. The purpose of giving this illustration is to show that those who deny that the Bible is inerrant have some grounds for doing so. Following his baptism Jesus spent forty days in the desert east of the Jordan River. During this time he was tempted. These temptations are recorded in two gospels, Matthew and Luke. Matthew (4:1-11) says that Jesus was first tempted to change stones into bread; then he was tempted to throw himself down from the temple; finally he was tempted to worship Satan. Luke (4:1-13) puts things differently. He says that Jesus was first tempted to change the stones into bread; then he was tempted to worship Satan; finally he was tempted to throw himself down from the temple.

The difficulty becomes clear when we ask ourselves the question: What was the order of Jesus' temptations? Frankly, I do not know.

We should notice several things about this example. For one thing, you do not have to be wicked and a hater of the Bible in order to feel the problem. Second, it is not unbelief or rationalism that brings on the problem; it is the text of the Bible. Another thing to notice is that the problem isn't very serious, since the real issue in the temptations is not their order but the fact that Jesus overcame them. Concerning what really matters there is no problem. Nevertheless the order of temptations differs. So we can see why some people say with good reason: "It looks to me like there is a mistake in the order in one of these records."

That is how the two positions are arrived at. The inerrancy position is supported by the fact that God must tell the truth; the errancy position is supported by the fact that some passages appear to have mistakes in them. I believe that the support for both sides is firm, so I shall have to try to reconcile them.

To reconcile these two views we must observe that *the inerrancy position is qualified by its proponents* in several important ways. People who affirm that the Bible is without error go on to qualify what they mean in different ways. I believe that when these qualifications are taken *seriously* they bring the inerrancy and errancy positions together. In other words, men who hold that the Bible does not err go on to say things of such a nature that they negate the differences between themselves and those who find errors in the Bible. Notice carefully that I am saying that the proponents, not the opponents, of inerrancy qualify what they mean by inerrancy.

I am going now to give four examples of qualifications of inerrancy made by people who believe in it. These qualifications, taken separately or together, constitute a major alteration in the basic inerrancy position. Perhaps there are others besides these four, but in any case these four will take us a long way toward seeing why the two apparently incompatible positions appear on closer investigation to be compatible.

The first qualification made by those who say the Bible is inerrant is that they are speaking only of the original manuscripts of the Bible, not of copies or translations. So far as I know, almost no one claims that the King James Version of the Bible is inerrant. Even modern critical texts are not inerrant, as you will see if you ask yourself the question: Which text of the New Testament is inerrant, the Westcott-Hort, the *Textus Receptus*, the United Bible Societies', the Nestle's, the Tasker, or the footnotes in the various texts? Proponents of inerrancy uniformly reply: No existing text is without error, only the original manuscripts, the autographs.

We cannot overestimate the importance of this qualification for reconciling the two positions. Those who accept inerrancy are talking about manuscripts *which do not exist today*; those who reject inerrancy are talking about the Bible *as we have it today.* They are speaking of two different realities. Little wonder they disagree on what to say about them.

What the proponents of inerrancy do say is that the Bible as we have it now is—not inerrant—but dependable. Here is Dr. Clark Pinnock's way of expressing this:

> It is common for Evangelicals to distinguish between the inspired originals or autographs and the uninspired copies or apographs . . . .
>
> A little reflection, however, reveals that the distinction is quite sound . . . . There is nothing absurd about an infallible text imperfectly transmitted . . . . If there is good evidence for the trustworthiness of the Bible as it came from the hand of God, and there is (the entire testimony of Christ and the apostles referred to above): and there is no evidence for the inspiration of copyists or translators, and there is none; then it follows quite logically that such a distinction must be made.[1]

Dr. Pinnock concludes this part of his book with this summary:

> Our Bibles are the Word of God to the extent that they reflect the Scripture as originally given; and because it is clear that they are virtually identical to it, it is also correct to regard them as virtually infallible themselves.[2]

The original manuscripts were "infallible;" the present texts are "virtually infallible." The difference which Dr. Pinnock makes here puts his position very close to that of those who say: As we read the Bible as we have it before us, there seem to be errors in it.

Furthermore, this qualification undercuts one of the

[1]Clark Pinnock, *Biblical Revelation*, pp. 81-82.

[2]*Ibid.*, p. 86.

arguments which I mentioned above. If the Bible as we now have it is "virtually infallible" rather than "infallible," then the argument which says that a solid faith requires a completely inerrant foundation does not apply. For if we build faith upon a foundation of the Bible, it must be the Bible as we now have it; we surely cannot literally depend on non-existent manuscripts. It is inconsistent to use this "foundation" argument unless you hold that some *existent* text is your foundation; in that case you will have to—or rather, you should want to—specify which text is inerrant.

A second qualification made by those who hold to inerrancy is that things are reported in the Bible as they appeared to the human authors. Events are reported phenomenologically, as they looked to the writer. So what is reported is what the writer *really* saw, though it may perhaps not be exactly what occurred. A recent adherent of inerrancy, Paul Little, has put it this way:

> For instance, the Scripture describes things phenomenalogically (*sic*)--that is as they *appear* to be. It speaks of the sun rising and setting. Now, we know that the sun does not actually rise and set, but that the earth rotates. But we use "sunrise" and "sunset" ourselves, even in an age of scientific enlightenment, because this is a convenient way of describing what appears to be. So we cannot charge the Bible with error when it speaks phenomenalogically (*sic*). Because it speaks in this way, it has been clear to men of all ages and cultures.
>
> In ancient times there were not the same standards of exactness in historical matters. Sometimes round numbers were used rather than precise figures. When the police estimate a crowd we know the figure is not accurate, but it is close enough for the purpose.[1]

It is clear that this qualification puts Mr. Little very close to those who see errors in the Bible, though he affirms there are none. He says that the Bible records things close enough for the purpose, and all Christians could affirm that. When such a

[1]Paul Little, *Know Why You Believe*, p. 35.

qualification as this is made, the area of disagreement between inerrancy and errancy had dwindled to nothing. No matter how much some may feel that there are still important differences, and no matter how different the positions sound, the difference now is either academic or non-existent.

A third qualification made by some proponents of inerrancy is that the writers of the Bible were preserved from error in what they taught but not in what they thought. While not all theologians who hold this view accept such a distinction some do.[1] The great theologian of orthodoxy at Princeton, Charles Hodge, wrote in his *Systematic Theology:*

> (The doctrine of plenary inspiration) denies that the sacred writers were merely partially inspired; it asserts that they were fully inspired as to all that they teach, whether of doctrine or fact. This of course does not imply that the sacred writers were infallible except for the special purpose for which they were employed. They were not imbued with plenary knowledge . . . . They were infallible only as teachers . . . . Isaiah was infallible in his predictions, although he shared with his countrymen the views then prevalent as to the mechanism of the universe. Paul could not err in anything he taught, although he could not recollect how many persons he had baptized in Corinth.[2]

Later on Hodge wrote:

> Do the sacred writers contradict each other? Do the Scriptures teach what from any source can be proved not to be true? The question is not whether the views of the sacred writers were incorrect, but whether they taught error? For example, it is not the question *whether* they thought that the earth is the centre of our system? but, Did they teach that it is?[3]

[1] Apparently Clark Pinnock has reversed his position on this point. In *A Defense of Biblical Infallibility* (1967), p. 14, he directly denied the position of Hodge. But in *Biblical Revelation* (1971), pp. 71-72, in calling attention to the "intended assertions of Scripture," in distinguishing subjects from terms, and in distinguishing what Scripture teaches from incidental references, he seems to accept Hodge's position.

[2] Charles Hodge, *Systematic Theology*, I, 165.

[3] *Ibid.*, p. 169.

Once again it is clear that this qualification helps reconcile the inerrancy and errancy positions. Inerrancy is not being claimed for the assumptions of the writer, or for his view of the universe, or for things he happens to mention incidentally, or for anything except what he consciously, deliberately intended to teach. That would help us see why, for example, the orders of the temptations of Jesus differ. Perhaps neither writer consciously concerned himself with the order; their only concern was to say that Jesus overcame the three temptations.

The fourth qualification made by those who hold to inerrancy is that the Bible does contain problems. Though their position rests on deductive arguments, they have read their Bibles inductively too, and they realize that some passages are difficult to understand. Here is how Dr. W. A. Criswell puts this qualification:

> The so-called errors of the Bible are a very slippery lot. Just when you think you have your hands on one it evades you and disappears. In essence, there are not errors but difficulties which can be solved or explained . . . .
>
> Difficulties in the Scripture do not overthrow their infallible nature. The difficulties are but mountains yet to be scaled and lands yet to be conquered.[1]

Dr. Criswell goes on to show how the difficulties arise, and he gives examples of apparent difficulties which have been resolved. He concludes his chapter by saying that the real difficulty we face is trying to acknowledge the greatness of God's power and love.

So when those who hold to inerrancy read the Bible, they see passages which they call "difficulties," while those who are not committed to inerrancy read the same passage, notice the same things that the inerrancy people do, and say: "Those look like mistakes to us." From this we see that the two groups see the same kinds of things when they read the Bible; they just describe them by different names.

[1]W. A. Criswell, *Why I Preach that the Bible is Literally True,* pp. 44-46.

I am convinced that since this is true, all that *really* separates these two groups of Christian brothers is a name, and names are not important enough to divide brothers in Christ. I do not think it matters what we *call* these passages. We could create a phrase and call them "the passages that have troubled brothers" or something. The point is that they are there; and we know it; although they are there, we have full confidence in the Good News which the Bible tells us; and we have too much in common to let these little things separate us. Unless we have come to the place that the Gospel is no longer enough to unite Christians, then I cannot see how we can avoid this conclusion.

If you put the four qualifications I mentioned together you can see how close inerrancy is to errancy.

The Bible is inerrant

1) not our translations or even modern texts but the original;

2) not in reporting things precisely but in reporting them as they appeared to the writers;

3) not in what the writers thought but only in which they directly taught;

4) and there are difficulties in the Bible.

Sometimes my students ask me which position I hold, that the Bible is inerrant or that it is not. When I think about these qualifications, I give them the only answer I can: I hold that the positions are virtually the same. And I draw an important conclusion: Let us quit fighting over this matter. Let us spend our energies affirming the Gospel which is the power of God unto salvation. Let us accept one another as brothers and live in peace so that others will want to join our family.

Now let us take up the second and more important question about the Bible: What shall we do with the Bible? It is less discussed because it is less controversial than the question of what we shall say about the Bible, but we must not let that fact deceive us into thinking that it is unimportant. The Bible is a medium by which God speaks to us; whether we get his message or not will depend in part upon what we do with the Bible. It is *very* important how we use it. We cannot affect what the Bible really is by what we say about it, but we will affect whether God speaks to us by what we do with the Bible. The Bible is God's Word whether we know it or not, but it will benefit us only if we listen properly. Walter Cronkite broadcasts the news whether we listen or not, but we do not learn about it unless we listen.

I do not think that the Bible is a magic book. I remember once hearing a story about a soldier whose life was saved because a bullet was stopped by a New Testament he carried in his shirt pocket. I am glad the bullet was stopped, but I agreed with a friend who said that a package of cigarettes might have done the same thing. The Bible is not a talisman; it is not magic. We do not carry it like a rabbit's foot or a lucky coin. Its presence does not make us more Christian or its absence make us less Christian.

Neither do we treat the Bible as a series of secret sayings. The Bible is open and clear in its message, and it is false to the Bible to look for hidden meanings. Biblical numerology simply misses the Gospel completely. Those who count the letters in the book of Genesis have simply by-passed the message of Genesis. Perhaps they have become bored with the message of the Bible, or perhaps they just have a penchant for arcane mysteries. Those who need esoteric teachings should read horoscopes not the Bible. The Bible tells quite openly about a God who is light, not darkness, and he is not playing games with us in his Word. The older Calvinistic theologians used to speak about the perspicuity of the Bible, and they were right. There may be some obscurities; after all the Bible is very old. But the great themes of the Bible are really open and clear, not hidden and obscure. The Baptist teaching about the priesthood of the believer means that each Christian can read the Bible for himself; no one teacher or sect has an edge on the truth of the Bible.

In fact, we do not read the Bible as a collection of sayings at all. It is not a collection of sayings, with the exception of the book of Proverbs. It has many genres (types of literature) in it, but very little of it is "sayings." And this means it must be read in context. One of my students once observed that a text out of context is a pretext, and he was right. The Bible is not written so that you may open to any page at random and find advice. You must give attention to what a passage meant to its original author and readers if you are to understand it properly.

When I was in college, some friends used to make fun of the method of reading the Bible which snatches a sentence out of its context and treats it as a "saying." They would quote a verse from the Old Testament which I still remember well: "At Parbar westward, four at the causeway, and two at Parbar" (I Chronicles 26:18). It is obvious to even the most mystically inclined person that this verse quoted alone means nothing. In fact, it does not sound like English at all. But in its context it has something to say.

If we read things in their context, quite often we get a very different understanding of what they mean. Take the words of Jesus:

> Enter by the narrow gate. The gate is wide that leads to perdition, there is plenty of room on the road, and many go that way; but the gate that leads to life is small and the road is narrow, and those who find it are few.
>
> (Matthew 7:13-14)

Read as a saying dropped from heaven, this passage seems clearly to say that God does not want many people to come to heaven, so he has fixed it so only a few can get in. But I do not think it means that at all. I think that Jesus looked around at the people in the cities and the country of Israel. What he saw there was a very few people who cared about God, and many people who did not care about God and so were lost. He reported, sadly I expect, the truth: few people are going to heaven. I am afraid that if he were living today he would observe the same thing.

We should not treat the Bible as an idol. We do this when we care more about it than we do about God who wrote it. Sometimes people ask what we believe in and we respond "the Bible." But that is not exactly true; we believe in God, the God who was in Christ, as we have read about him in the Bible. The Bible is a means to the end that we have faith in God; if we make an end in itself, then we make it an idol. God is the end; the Bible is a means through which God speaks to us.

Neither do we defend the Bible. We study it for ourselves and we proclaim its message to others, but we do not defend it. God is more likely to use the Bible to defend us and our faith than he is to use us to defend the Bible. I like the saying attributed to the great Baptist preacher of London, Charles Haddon Spurgeon: "Defend the Bible? I had as soon defend a lion."

What we do with the Bible is to study and read it. We study it in the most rigorous intellectual way we can. We study it from the perspective of faith in Christ, but not mindlessly. We study it regularly and thoughtfully. We are alert for God's Word to us, but not in a private or superstitious way. As the drama of the Bible comes before us, we listen for God's Word; we look for God's act. Most important, we take our stand upon the Gospel, asking how we shall understand what is said in the Bible in view of our conviction that God was in Christ reconciling.

The Southern Baptist Convention first adopted the statement of faith called *The Baptist Faith and Message* in 1925. When that statement was revised for readoption in 1963, only one major change was made in the article entitled "The Scriptures." This was the addition of a final sentence which read: "The criterion by which the Bible is to be interpreted is Jesus Christ." This is what I mean when I say we should read the Bible in the light of the Gospel. We must give to the Gospel the priority which it deserves. We must read the Bible as those who have faith in Jesus Christ. This is our basic hermeneutical principle: Jesus Christ. If we take Jesus as our criterion for interpreting the Bible, it will not solve all our problems. It will not make interpretation easier or rigorous study less necessary, but it will make our understanding of the Bible more Christian.

Other criteria have been suggested. We noted in Chapter One that some people today read the Bible in terms of dispensationalism; their chief hermeneutical principle is the dispensational scheme. The late E. J. Carnell of Fuller Theological Seminary suggested that we read the Bible in the light of the principle of justification by faith.[1] But I think it is better to take Christ, who was the fullest revelation of God, as the criterion for understanding the Bible.

If we do this, then perhaps the Bible could become "the true center of Christian union" of which the *Baptist Faith and Message* spoke. This is the conviction of at least some theologians. Geoffrey Bromiley of Fuller Seminary has written:

> We may go to the Bible with very different views of what it is and how it is to be understood or applied. But if we go primarily to see Christ (John 5:39), i.e., to learn what the Bible has to tell us about Him, and our new life in Him, we shall be brought together at the one true center of the church and its unity.[2]

I agree. More important than anything else we have to say about the Bible is this: we must read it as those who believe that God was in Christ reconciling, listening for God to continue to speak to us.

In summary, we need for God to speak to us if we are to know him. He has graciously spoken to us through various media. He has revealed himself as creator through the world he made, and he has revealed himself as savior through events in history, especially in the history of Israel which reached its climax in Jesus Christ. He speaks to us also through the

[1]E. J. Carnell, *The Case for Orthodox Theology*, chapter 4.
[2]Geoffrey Bromiley, *The Unity and Disunity of the Church*, p. 69.

Bible, which tells us about the Gospel. Christians who fight over what to say about certain passages in the Bible should be reconciled because their positions, when they are qualified, are not incompatible and, in any case, they are brothers who all believe that God was in Christ reconciling. We should spend our efforts studying the Bible and trying to hear the Word which God speaks to us there, a message which is truth without any mixture of error.

For further reading:

The theologian who gave to revelation its prominence in twentieth century theology was Karl Barth. For the story of that important event see John Baillie, *The Idea of Revelation in Recent Thought*. There have been debates about whether there is a revelation through nature; Baillie deals with that also. For a clear though overstated presentation of revelation through history see G. Ernest Wright, *God Who Acts*. The tension between faith and history is spelled out in Van A. Harvey's *The Historian and the Believer*. The book which I feel is destined to become a classical statement of the case for inerrancy (and that is not its only importance) is Clark Pinnock's *Biblical Revelation*. Among Southern Baptists this issue may be canvassed in W. A Criswell's *Why I Preach that the Bible is Literally True* and in *Is the Bible a Human Book?* edited by Wayne E. Ward and Joseph F. Green.

3. GOD

Introduction

This chapter is the first of four in which I shall deal directly with the doctrine of God. In it I intend to speak mainly of God as he is revealed in the Old Testament and of the relationship between the Old Testament understanding of God and the views held by some philosophers.

Whenever we try to say what we mean by "God," we must realize that we cannot say everything; some things must be left out. All that we can do is to select the most important things we know of as we speak about God.

I will begin by saying that the word "God" refers to one who is personal and transcendent. I shall then say that God is good and loving. In doing this I shall be following a scheme similar but not identical to the one in older theologies which spoke first of God's nature and then of his attributes.

God is Personal and Transcendent

To affirm that God is personal is to use an analogy drawn from everyday experience. Almost all men make a common sense distinction between persons and things. We are not born with this distinction, but we develop it while we are young, and it is deeply ingrained in us. Children learn early to respond to parents in one way and to toys in another. The distinction is not always clear in their minds; they may personify a doll or a teddy bear. Live pets present even more of a difficulty because they sometimes behave in ways that encourage children to treat them as persons. But eventually we sort these things out, and most of us hold to the distinction between persons and things in a fairly consistent way. We are amused by adults who treat their pets literally like persons, and we are offended by insensitive people who manipulate and abuse persons as if they were things. We believe that morality requires us to treat persons as persons, to have only I-Thou relationships with them.[1] Though we do not always live up to this demand, we do have some idea about why we believe in it.

To speak of God as personal is to assume that the common sense distinction between persons and things is accurate. It is then to affirm that God is more like a person than like a thing. He is more like a father than like a doll or toy or pet.

Transcendence is basically a spatial analogy. It has to do with a location in space. Something is transcendent if it is above other things. To transcend is to be higher. We also use "transcendent" to describe non-spatial relations. For example, a person may transcend his surroundings. This means that, breaking away from an environment that might have tied him down, he finds a freedom he might otherwise not have known. So when we are affirming God's transcendence, we are saying that he is above the world and that he is free from confinement of any sort.

Now you can see why I wanted to link "personal" with "transcendent." They balance each other. To say that God is both personal and transcendent is to say that he is both like us and unlike us. He is more like a person than a rock, yet he transcends persons as we understand them.

There are many testimonies to the personhood and transcendence of God. One that we do not always recognize is our religious consciousness. In the feelings and intuitions of religious people there is often a sense that God is both very close and very far away. This intuition was described incisively by Rudolf Otto in his book *The Idea of the Holy*. He described a religious man's sense of God as a *mysterium*

[1]The term "I-Thou" was created by Martin Buber, a Jewish philosopher, to describe the kind of mutually personal relations of which I am speaking above. This term has been widely adopted by Christian writers. Buber's book, *I and Thou*, was published in 1923.

tremendum et fascinans, a tremendous yet fascinating mystery. My way of putting this double sense is to say that God is both winsome and awesome. We are drawn to him because he is like us, personal; we feel awe before him because he is unlike us, transcendent.

As Otto points out, this understanding of God is found in the Bible. Throughout the Bible God is spoken of as personal. Although the biblical writers use impersonal metaphors (fortress, light), they all believed that God was personal. The Bible contains many anthropomorphisms which have offended some people, but if we allow other passages from the Bible to balance them then they should not trouble us. The other passages I refer to are those which speak of God's holiness. "Holy" did not originally mean good; its basic meaning was "separate." God is the separate one, the different one. He is different from all creation; he is different from man too. The anthropomorphisms in the Bible are balanced by the affirmation that God is holy. He is like us yet unlike us; he is personal and transcendent.

Now we need to examine some of the implications of God's personal and transcendent dimensions. I am going to take the personal dimension first, because I believe that today we face more difficulty with it than we do with God's transcendence. I shall explain this as I go along.

To say that God is personal is to communicate that he is real. What is like us is real to us; what is different from us often has an air of unreality about it. To affirm that God is real is not to affirm that he has a body or anything like that, but it is to say that we are not talking about an abstraction or an ideal or a function of human religious consciousness. We are saying that Someone is there. In traditional terms, we are affirming theism and denying atheism. Atheism is the denial that there is a God. We believe atheists are wrong. There is a God.

Some Christians think that no one is really an atheist. This is not exactly true. There are people who are convinced that there is no creator, no life after death, all values are imaginary, there is no spiritual dimension to life, no point to life, and religion is an illusion. Perhaps at times they do not live up to their negative creed, but this is their creed nevertheless, and it is atheistic. In the past atheism was a rare stance, held only by a few advanced thinkers. Today it is more widespread. This has been documented by the psychoanalyst Ignace Lepp in his book *Atheism in our Time*.

Some Christians have tried to wed atheism to Christian faith. Thomas Altizer's *The Gospel of Christian Atheism* is one such attempt. I think these efforts fail because Christianity is irrevocably committed to the position that God is real. This means that Christians reject atheism.

We need to say one thing more about the reality of God. It is very important to Christian faith. It is important objectively, in that faith and worship and prayer make no sense unless there is a God toward whom they are directed. And the reality of God is important subjectively. We feel that God is real, and this feeling is very important to us. We believe there really is a God. People sometimes suppose that we speak of God because we think that such ideas are helpful or are good for us, but this is not exactly true. We speak of God because there is a God. Quite often people are surprised to learn that we do not say God is real simply because it is sweet or good for our children or a heritage we value but because it is so. In modern philosophical terms, we make a truth-claim, we assert a fact, when we say that God is real.

To say that God is personal means also that he is living. He is not dead. He is not an abstraction or a value or a thing, but a living, personal reality. This is why religion is a personal relationship; God is living and personal, and we can relate to him in a living personal way. Anything other than a personal relationship does not correspond with what God is. So the fact that God is living and personal is very important for our religious faith and practice.

Throughout the Bible God is pictured as living. He is called the living God in contrast to idols worshiped by pagans. In the following passage the writer ridicules idols made of clay and then warns those who worship them of their fate. He begins with a reference to the fact that the true God is not in one place, visible and physical, like an idol located above an altar in a temple.

Why do the nations ask,
 Where then is their God?
Our God is in high heaven;
 He does whatever pleases Him.
Their idols are silver and gold,
 made by the hands of men.
They have mouths that cannot speak,
 and eyes that cannot see;
They have ears that cannot hear,
 nostrils, and cannot smell;
With their hands they cannot feel,
 with their feet they cannot walk,
 and no sound comes from their throats.
Their makers grow to be like them,
 and so do all who trust in them. (Psalm 115:2-8)

The writer is using irony when he observes that idols, though they are physical, are dead and so unreal; the true God, though not physical, is living and so he is the real God.

Because God is a living personal God, he can act in human history. The Psalmist was ridiculing idols because they are ineffective, they don't do anything; God can act, and he does.

When we say that God can act in this way, we are denying a position called deism. At about the time of the French Revolution a number of writers took the position that God had created the world but then had withdrawn and was no longer related to the world. These men were called deists. Although the name is seldom applied to our contemporaries, there are still many people who, for all practical purposes, are deists. They do not perceive God as being active in the world today, and they are not at all sure that he ever acted in the world. As we saw in Chapter Two, Christians believe that God is active in history. We note that in affirming the personhood of God we affirm the possibility that God may act.

In summary, we say that since God is personal he is real (against atheism), living (against idolatry), and active in our world (against deism). Now let us consider more fully what it means to say that God is transcendent.

The transcendence of God, his separateness, stands in contrast to a teaching known as pantheism, which holds that the word "God" is a name for the sum total of everything that exists. In other words, for pantheists God is the All; he is "Universe" with a capital "U." But the Christian view denies this and affirms that God is not to be identified with the universe. He is not all or part of the universe but is other than it.

This is spelled out most clearly in the Christian teaching that God is the creator of the universe. It is well known that the Bible opens with the majestic phrase: "In the beginning God created the heavens and the earth." The theme of creation appears repeatedly in the Bible. The name given to this teaching among philosophers is *creatio ex nihilo*, creation out of nothing. This phrase goes back to a sentence in an ancient Jewish book that is not found in Protestant Bibles (it is in Catholic Bibles):

> I beg you, child, look at the sky and the earth;
> see all that is in them and realize that God made
> them out of nothing, and that man comes into being
> in the same way. (II Macc. 7:28)

When a Latin translation of this book appeared it rendered the words "out of nothing" as *ex nihilo*, and the phrase has stayed with us.

When we say that God has created the world we are affirming at least four sets of facts.

1. We are saying something about the relations between God and the world.

2. We are saying something about God.

3. We are saying something about the world generally.

4. We are saying something about man particularly.

The fourth group is the most controversial because it seems to contradict the scientific theories of evolution. I shall discuss the creation of man in Chapter Four.

We shall begin with the relationship between God and the world. Let us consider together three situations. One is an ocean, made up of billions of drops of water. The second is the sun with sunbeams streaming out from it in all directions. The third is an autograph party at which a novelist is signing copies of his new book. Each of these situations can serve as an analogy for the relationship between God and the universe. Things in the world may be drops in the great ocean called God. That is pantheism. Or things may be streams of God moving away from God, like sunbeams from the sun. This view of the world is called emanationism, and it was held by many pagan people in the first century when Christianity was born. Or things in the world may be something other than God, existing because he created them, as a novel exists because the novelist created it. That is the Christian view, and it is called creation.

So creation is one analogy among several which have from time to time been proposed to describe the relationship between God and the world. The analogy is spelled out in this passage from the Old Testament:

> All this I, the Lord, have created.
> Will the pot contend with the potter,
> or the earthen ware with the hand that shapes it?
> Will the clay ask the potter what he is making?
> or his handiwork say to him, 'You have no skill?'
> Will the babe say to his father, 'What are you begetting?'
> or to his mother, 'What are you bringing to birth?'
> Thus says the Lord, Israel's Holy One, his maker:

Would you dare question me concerning my children,
Or instruct me in my handiwork?
I alone, I made the earth
and created man upon it;
I with my own hands, stretched out the heavens
and caused all their hosts to shine. (Isaiah 45:8-12)

The writer has employed three metaphors to describe creation: a potter making a pot, a parent having a child, and a camper putting up his tent. All three of these say that God made the world, and that is very different from the idea that the world is a part of God or an emanation from God.

Second, what does creation say to us about God? It tells us that he is other than the world, as a potter is other than his pottery. It tells us that he is not be be confused with the world or the world with him. It tells us that God is independent of the world.

It also tells us that God is unique. He is responsible for the existence of everything in creation. This means that there cannot be two or more gods. There is only one. Creation implies monotheism. Belief in many gods (polytheism) is not compatible with belief in creation. Few people today are polytheistic in their belief, but many are polytheistic in their practice. They move through life switching their allegiance from one god to another. But there is only one true God, maker of all things visible and invisible.

Third, what does creation tell us about the world? It says that the world is not the same as God nor is it a part of God. The world is not to be confused with God or to be regarded as divine. The world is dependent upon God, since it could not exist unless he made it, just as a novel would not exist unless a novelist wrote it. In other words, the world is both independent of God (other than God) and dependent upon God. This apparent contradiction might bother us if we did not bear in mind that the same things must be said about a novel and its writer. The book is independent of (other than) the writer yet dependent upon the writer, apart from whom it would not exist. I call this a relative independence, in distinction from the absolute independence of God.

Finally, creation tells us that the importance and purpose of the world reside in God. For a Christian the question "What is the meaning of life?" can be restated as "What is God's purpose for human life?" The purpose behind a novel is the novelist's purpose for it, and the purpose behind the world is God's purpose for it. Later on we shall try to say what that purpose is.

There is one aspect of the divine creation which cannot be found in human analogies, and that is the *ex nihilo*. We men can never create out of nothing; to create we must make use of materials, experiences, and ideas which come to us from outside ourselves. God does not; he does not utilize anything outside himself for creation. It is good to remind ourselves of this since it fixes in our minds the fact that creation, like all truth about God, is an analogy.

So transcendence means that God is separate from the world and also creator of the world. It also means that God is free. He is free from the limitations of space that we have; we can be at only one place at a time, but God is not confined by space. He is free from the limitations of time. Our existence on earth is limited by birth and death. Limitations of space and time do not apply to God, yet he is also free to act within the world of space and time.

God is also free from any limitations of power or knowledge. He never lacks the power or knowledge to achieve his intended goals. Yet he is free voluntarily to restrain his power and knowledge in order to achieve purposes that call for such restraint.

We have been saying that God is personal (real, living, and active) and transcendent (holy, Creator, and free). Many thoughtful persons today find it difficult to say that God can be personal and also be free from all limitations. They ask if it is not necessary for persons to have limitations. Could there be a person with no limits? If God transcends all limits, does not he transcend the distinction between the personal and the non-personal? Here is how a philosopher, C. C. J. Webb, expressed it:

> A modern controversy about 'the personality of God' will be found to turn upon the difficulty involved in reconciling the finitude which seems to be essential to human personality with the absoluteness and infinity, or at least omnipresence and omnipotence, which we are accustomed to ascribe to God.[1]

This problem brings us for the first time to one of the larger issues in contemporary theology. The issue is this: We have a Jewish-Christian heritage which always thinks of God in personal, even anthropomorphic, terms. On the other hand there is the Greek philosophical heritage which generally dismisses personal ideas of God as superstitious and in their place puts an abstraction called (among other things) the Absolute. Early in Christian history these two heritages came into contact with each other. It was difficult for Christian theologians to know what to do with the Greek heritage. They felt that they had many things in common with Plato, for example, such as respect for moral values like truth, courage, and honesty; certainly they felt closer to him than they did to pagans whose philosophy was "eat, drink, and be merry." Yet Plato did not believe in a personal God. The frustration that resulted from the conflict between Christian faith in a personal God and philosophical abstractions was summed up by Tertullian, an African theologian, when he asked: "What has Athens to do with Jerusalem?" We still have that conflict and feel that frustration today.

In the twentieth century theologians have taken three different positions on the problem of relating God's personhood to his transcendence. One group of men, called personalists, has said that God is personal but not absolute. The great attractiveness of this position arises from its ability to answer the problem of evil. To those who ask why, if God is all-powerful, he does not destroy all undeserved suffering, the personalists responded that he is not *all*-powerful. He is

[1]C. C. J. Webb, *Problems in the Relations of God and Man*, p. 216.

very powerful, and he is at work defeating evil, but tnere are limits to what he can do. I do not think that the personalists have influenced many people, though perhaps they have.

Other Christian thinkers have affirmed that God is absolute but not personal. Among these we would include the late Dr. Paul Tillich. Instead of speaking of God as personal he spoke of "the ground of being." In a small book entitled *Biblical Religion and the Search for Ultimate Reality*, he sharply contrasted the philosopher's quest with the religious man's faith. He concluded that both spoke of a transcendent reality. But he described that reality in non-personal terms.

> The God who is *a* being is transcended by the God who is Being itself, the ground and abyss of every being. And the God who is *a* person is transcended by the God who is the Personal-Itself, the ground and abyss of every person.[1]

I do not know exactly what Dr. Tillich meant by "ground and abyss," but I feel sure that he did not mean the same thing that ordinary Christians mean when they think of God as personal. I am happy, though puzzled, that Dr. Tillich continued to affirm that we men stand in an I-Thou relationship to God in spite of the impersonal language he used in talking about God.

The third position is that God is both personal and transcendent, and I have taken that position. Though there are difficulties in it, I am convinced that it is the true one. As I stated above, I think that both the Bible and religious experience support this position. And I believe that a coherent picture can be given of the two seemingly diverse elements. We can say simply that God is both like and unlike ourselves. This is not a completely unusual statement, since we are accustomed to speaking of one person as both like and unlike another person. In a much greater way God is like and unlike all men.

The great problem which this position faces is the problem of evil. If God is personal, then he cares about us and wants to save us from all suffering and evil. If he is transcendent,

[1]Paul Tillich, *Biblical Religion and the Search for Ultimate Reality*, pp. 82-83.

then he is able to save us from suffering and evil. But suffering and evil exist. Therefore, either God is not personally concerned or he is not transcendently powerful.

This logic is very strong, and Christians must try to give some response to the problem. Of all the difficulties that men have with faith in God, this is the greatest. Perhaps it always has been; it was a real problem to Job in the Old Testament. We shall try to respond to it in chapters six and eleven.

We have said that God is personal and transcendent. Now we must ask, "What kind of God is he?" This is similar to a question we might ask about any personal being unlike ourselves: "What is he like?" In traditional theological language, this is the question of the attributes or perfections of God.

God is Good and Loving

In the past theologians have sometimes drawn up long lists of qualities which, they say, are descriptive of God. Thus Louis Berkhof, a Presbyterian theologian, follows a long tradition when he lists the attributes of God as self-existence, immutability, infinity, unity, spirituality, intellectual and moral qualities, and sovereignty.[1] It is also traditional to classify these attributes into groups like moral attributes and metaphysical attributes.

I expect that most Christians would be able to agree with these descriptions. I do. But they leave me uneasy because they sound unreal. We do not describe real people around us in this way. Have you ever heard anyone say: "This is my wife Hilda. She is characterized by moral qualities like industriousness, fortitude, patience, and by physical attributes like petiteness, cleanliness, and youthfulness"? My feeling is that all this sounds as "phoney" when it is used of God as it does when it is used of a human being.

What can we do to restore reality to the adjectives? Or, to put it differently, can we describe God in a way that is consonant with the reality of God? I think we can. One step toward doing this is to avoid the classifications of attributes.

[1]Louis Berkof, *Systematic Theology*, chapters 5-7.

Another is to reduce the list to manageable length. When we remember that no list can be comprehensive, it does not seem too daring of us to be selective. But we do bear the responsibility for whatever list we make, and that is part of the burden that comes to anyone who thinks about God for himself.

I elect to speak of God as good and loving. These two qualities of God seem to me to be the most important ones that I know of. Perhaps in some way they contain within themselves many of the others like patience or justice, though I shall not try to develop this now. Perhaps religious instinct leads me to select these two. Perhaps it is the enormous volume of the biblical revelation about them which directs me to them. For whatever reasons, these two qualities seem to me to stand out from the rest.

We begin by noting that both of them are analogies drawn from the personal lives and relations of human beings. To affirm God's goodness is to say this: "You see those two politicians? One of them is a crook and the other is not. One cannot be trusted and the other can. One is bad and the other is good. God is like the good one, not like the bad one." To affirm God's love is to say this: "You see those two women there? Both have children. One is glad she has children, the other regrets her children. One concerns herself for the welfare of her children, the other ignores her children. One cares for her children in every possible way, the other is indifferent to her children. God is like the loving mother, not like the unloving one."

It is a false analogy to say that God is like a crooked politician or an indifferent mother. It is a true analogy to say that God is like an honest politician or a caring mother. These analogies of goodness and love can be qualified if we say that God is not good or loving in precisely the same way that politicians and mothers are (*via negationis*), since he is better than any human being could ever be and he loves more than any human being could ever love (*via eminentia*).

The Bible contains many references to the goodness of God.

One of the clearest of these is the concern of the Old Testament prophets for righteousness. In their day many people in Israel felt that God's primary concern was for sacrifices, festivals, prayers, and other rituals. The prophets insisted that God's real concern was moral not ritual. Here is how Amos put it:

Seek good and not evil,
  that you may live,
that the Lord the God of Hosts may be finally on your side,
  as you say he is.
Hate evil and love good;
  enthrone justice in the courts;
  it may be that the Lord the God of Hosts
  will be gracious to the survivors of Joseph.

I hate, I spurn your pilgrim-feasts;
  I will not delight in your sacred ceremonies.
When you present your sacrifices and offerings,
  I will not accept them,
  nor look on the buffaloes of your shared-offerings.
  Spare me the sound of your songs;
  I cannot endure the music of your lutes.
  Let justice roll on like a river
  and righteousness like an ever-flowing stream.
(Amos 5:14-15, 21-24)

Now if God wants men to be good, just, and righteous, it is because he is that way. He is not capriciously waiting to see who will offer a sacrifice in the proper manner; he wants us to treat people fairly. He is not as interested in our saying beautiful prayers as he is in our telling the truth.

The importance of this prophetic revelation of God as good cannot be overestimated. Perhaps it is not too much to say that it marks the end of superstition, thereby providing a foundation for religion and society as we know them in Western civilization. Even so, the prophetic message that God is good was not the final word on that subject. The final word came in Jesus, and we shall give attention to this in chapters five and six.

Today men tend to affirm God's goodness formally but not to believe in it deeply. Sometimes they are troubled by Christian teachings about judgment and hell. They ask: "Can God judge men this way and really be good?" In Chapter Eleven I shall say something about judgment, but now I want to emphasize that God really is good; he always does what is right. We can trust him never to do wrong, and, in fact, if we do not believe and believe deeply that he is good, then all our religious life is in error, for faith in God's goodness is a fundamental element in our religion.

Now let us consider what the Bible says about the love of God. In the Old Testament the most dramatic witness to God's love is the story of the prophet Hosea and his wife Gomer. Gomer was a prostitute, perhaps engaged in religious prostitution in connection with the worship of the idol Baal. But Hosea loved her in spite of her promiscuity.

> The Lord said to me,
> Go again and love a woman
> loved by another man, an adulteress,
> and love her as the Lord loves the Israelites
> although they resort to other gods
> and love the raisin-cakes offered to their idols.
> So I got her back for fifteen pieces of silver, a homer of barley and a measure of wine: and I said to her, many a long day you shall live in my house.
>
> (Hosea 3:1-3)

What we see here is simply the concern of the prophet for Gomer. She was important to him. He worked to overcome everything that separated her from him and to unite her with himself. He cared for her welfare. The message of Hosea is that this is how God loves men. They are important to him. He works to overcome everything that separates them from him and to unite them to himself. He cares for their welfare.

As wonderful as this revelation of God's love is, especially for guilty men who feel unworthy of the love of God, the prophetic message was not the final word on God's love. The final word came with Jesus Christ, and we shall discuss it further in chapters five, six, and eight.

Let us conclude this chapter with a brief review. Remembering that our language is analogical, we have affirmed that, like ourselves, God is personal, though he is also very different from ourselves. We have said that this transcendent personal God is good and loving. We can trust in One who does what is right, in One who loves and is concerned about us. This great faith, shared as it is by Jews and Christians, is a light in our dark world. It brings meaning into the chaos in which we live. It is the best way of seeing the world and of coping with life's problems.

It is not easy to trust in God. Contrary to popular belief, real faith has never been easy. Many things in our world speak against it, especially the misery of much of man's life. We need now to turn our attention to man and his predicament and then to ask whether, in view of our awful predicament, we can still believe that there is a God who loves us.

For further reading:

For a strong case for thinking about God as personal and for a clear presentation of the doctrine of creation, see Leonard Hodgson, *For Faith and Freedom*, Volume I. Paul Tillich's *Biblical Religion and the Search for Ultimate Reality* is an attempt to reconcile the personal and non-personal views which seems to me to lose the former. Gustaf Aulen rejects some of the categories of transcendence in the name of biblical theology in *The Drama and the Symbols*. Fr. John Courtney Murray's *The Problem of God* spells out the three perspectives of the Bible, the Fathers, and the modern world. The love of God is discussed in *Agape and Eros* by Anders Nygren; his methodology is questionable, but the influence of his thesis is very widespread. There are other studies of the love of God by John McIntyre, Daniel Day Williams, and John Burnaby. The modern man's dilemma about God is discussed by Langdon Gilkey in *Naming the Whirlwind*.

4. MAN

Introduction

In the twentieth century an enormous amount of attention is being devoted to man. History, biography, anthropology, sociology, and psychology, are all studies of human beings. Add to them our preoccupation with politics, our attention to finance and economics, our concern about education and health, the time we spend reading fiction and biography and watching drama, and you begin to see that most of man's attention is directed towards himself.

Why then should we who are trying to think about God add anything to the mountain of words that have been written about man? The answer is that we have something to say that is not being said by others. We try to speak of man in relation to God. In this chapter we will consider man in two of his relationships with God. First, man is a creation of God. Second, man is a sinner before God.

I want to be very clear on one point before I begin to explain what these two relationships mean. The man of whom I am speaking is not someone who exists only in my mind; I am speaking about the real people on the earth. The real people who drive cars, spend money, fall in love, read books, raise children, play games, and try to make sense out of their lives—they are creations of God, and they are sinners before God. It is important that we understand that these two relationships with God obtain not only for Christian people but for all human beings. Everyone is a creation of God, and everyone is a sinner before God.

Men Are Creations of God

We have already spoken of God as creator. Now we speak about the fact that men are creations of God. Usually when we refer to this fact we think of the story of the creation of Adam and Eve in the early chapters of Genesis. This is proper and natural, but we must not slip into the idea that only Adam was a creation of God. Creation is a present reality as well as a past reality. Not only Adam and Eve, but all men are creations of God. It does not matter if a man is a communist, a primitive tribesman, a very wicked person, an atheist, or a Muslim, he is God's creation.

Now you may say: "People are born because of the sexual union of their parents. So in what sense do you mean that they are God's creation?" To answer that question we must remember that creation is an analogy. God is the creator of a child who is born in a maternity ward today just as he was the creator of Adam long ago. In both cases creation is a true analogy. Just as a potter is responsible for the existence of his pottery, so God is responsible for the existence of Adam and of every person today. The fact that we are conceived by our parents and born nine months later does not affect our relationship with God at all. God does not act only when we people are inactive, nor does he become inactive just because we are active. Certainly in a true sense children are born of their parents; also in a true sense they are created by God. These two facts function in different dimensions. Both are real, and both are important.

We are accustomed to explain other events in our world in terms of different dimensions. For example, a football game may be described physically in terms of the size and speed of the players, or strategically in terms of the game plans of the two teams, or personally in terms of the ambition of the coaches or the commitment and perseverance of individual players. These different dimensions—the physical, the strategic, the personal—are all real, and they are all important. If it takes several dimensions to tell the story of a football game, we should not be surprised that it takes several dimensions to tell the story of the meaning of a human life.

So babies are born of their parents, and they are created by God. To this fact we now add that not only at birth but throughout his life each person is a creation of God. This means that my existence from one moment to the next rests upon the creative activity of God. To put it another way, my relationship to God is that he always is sustaining my life. We do not always feel sustained by God, but our feelings do not affect the relationship. I may eat, rest, exercise, and take medicine so that I may continue to live, and that is an important dimension of my life; another important dimension is that God is continuously sustaining my life.

We said that God is good and loving, so it follows that whatever he creates is good. That is confirmed by the Bible which says that "God saw all that he had made, and it was very good" (Genesis 1:30). In their minds many Christians know that they are good creations of God, but they do not feel it in their emotions. They feel that there is something wrong not only with their sins (we shall discuss this in a moment) but just with being themselves. The youngster who asks "What is wrong with me?" and the youth who says "I am different and I hate it" do not feel emotionally that they are good creations of God, however well they may understand it intellectually. It is also possible to deny the goodness of God's creation in other ways as, for example, by reckoning the importance of a person's life by how much money or possessions he has, or by how much power he influences over others, or by the level of society into which he was born. We must learn to evaluate a person's worth in terms of his relationship with God and to affirm that it is good to be what God has made us.

We see this clearly in works of fiction. I do not have much natural interest in Cuban fishermen, but I read Ernest Hemingway's *Old Man and the Sea* without stopping for a break. I have no concern about the lives of middle-class French countrywomen of the nineteenth century, but I was spellbound by Gustave Flaubert's *Madame Bovary*. I became involved in the lives of two fictional characters very unlike myself. Why was this? It was because I saw them through the eyes of their creators. They became important to me because of what their creators made them to be. The analogy is clear: Human beings are important because God is their maker.

Being creations of God not only means that people are important. It also means that they are limited and finite. We are not our own makers. Our lives had a beginning, and they will have a conclusion. There are limits to what we can understand, feel, and achieve. Because of our finitude, there are times in all our lives when we are powerless to alter bad situations. We are products of the era and country in which we live. We are affected by the history which preceded us and by the forces which whirl around us. As creations of God, we have real limitations.

We have said that every person begins and continues his life as a creation of God, that it is good to be such persons, and that as creations of God our lives have limits.

Now we want to see how we are related to the other creations of God, namely, to nature. Our relationship is dual: we have some things in common with other creations, but we are also unique. Both these facts are important, and we must not allow either to cancel out the other.

We have physical things in common with nature, of course. But our being a part of nature is more than a matter of our bodies. In particular we have things in common with other animals, especially with the higher animals. Contemporary investigations like Dr. Jane Goodall's study of chimpanzees show us that other animals have primitive social organization somewhat similar to our social structures. They also communicate, as we do, with signs and sounds. They have primitive feelings of anger, fear, and so on. The similarities between men and other animals are striking.

Some Christians are threatened by our similarities with

animals. I do not feel, however, that we should be threatened by them. The question is not whether there are similarities between men and animals; there are. The question is whether there are any differences. In my judgment, that is why the controversies about evolution were so misleading. I will explain what I mean by telling a little about the famous Scopes trial.

In the 1920's many states, Tennessee among them, had a law against teaching evolution in public schools. In Dayton, Tennessee, in 1925 a young high school science teacher named John Scopes decided to test the constitutionality of the law, so he asked leaders in Dayton to come hear him teach evolution in the high school. Subsequently he was put on trial for breaking the law and was defended by the famous attorney Clarence Darrow. The equally famous William Jennings Bryan, three times a candidate for President of the United States and an impressive orator, prosecuted the case. The trial was carried on radio all across America, which is one reason it became so famous; it was one of the first public events to be broadcast nationwide.

The trial had many fasinating moments. Darrow quipped that he had seen Bryan, an enormous man, consume gargantuan breakfasts and then sally forth to preach temperance. During the trial, Darrow was giving geological evidence to support the idea that the Bible was wrong in its estimate of the age of the earth, to which Bryan responded: "I am more interested in the Rock of Ages than in the age of rocks." Bryan won the case; Scopes was found guilty and given a minor fine. The antievolution laws stayed on the books of Tennessee and other states for many years, though most states have repealed them in the past few years.

The trial produced quotable sayings but not much careful thought. It is my judgment that Bryan and Darrow shared a mistaken presupposition. Both assumed that if you know the ancestry of man, you know his importance. Darrow thought that if he could prove that men came from monkeys or that men and monkeys had a common ancestor, he would have demonstrated that man is not made "in God's image." Bryan felt that he must prove that men did not come from such ancestors, or else the biblical view that man was made in God's image would be lost. I think both of them were wrong. You do not demonstrate the worth of man by demonstrating his ancestors. For that matter, you do not demonstrate the worth of anything by spelling out its origins.

Logicians have named this error the genetic fallacy. It is the fallacy of supposing that to know the ancestry of anything is to know its worth. You do not know the truth or falsity of a statement because you know who made it. You do not know the worth of a man because you know who his parents are. You do not know the value of a book because you know its author or publisher. Lowly origins prove nothing; neither do noble origins. A thing must be evaluated for itself.

The fact that man may have had lowly origins does not prove that man was not made in God's image. The Bible itself speaks of man being made from dust; that is a very lowly origin. Adam was not less important a creation of God because he was made from dust. The physical origins of all people are modest. Each of us began as the union of two tiny cells in our mother's body. That is not a grand beginning, but it does not change the fact that men come to be much more than that union, that they are important, and that they are made in God's image.

That is the real issue: Not whether we began modestly, but whether we have moved beyond modest beginnings. The question is not whether we are like monkeys, but whether that is all that we are. The question is not whether we are animals but whether we are merely animals. To say that our origin proves that we are "nothing but" animals is to engage in reductionism, and it is a logical mistake. Both Bryan and Darrow committed the genetic fallacy, and so their debate is not a good guide for us. As for the question of man's origins, that is a scientific matter to be worked on by people trained to do that. In my judgment the outcome of that discussion does not at all affect the Christian affirmation that man is a creation of God. Scientists examine how our world functions; Christians talk about what our world means. However man may function and whatever his origins, the meaning of his life rests in his relationship with God. He is made by God in God's image.

It is in the book of Genesis that the uniqueness of man is described as the "image of God" (Genesis 1:26-27). This phrase is frequently employed in Christian theology and preaching, and many debates have been conducted about its precise meaning. Some have argued that it refers to man's power of speech. Others say it is his reason. Others believe it refers to his awareness of moral values. Some feel that it is man's capacity for knowing God. One recent theologian, Karl Barth, has argued that it was the potential for interpersonal relationships of which male and female is a prototype. These different views were possible for a simple reason: The Bible does not tell us precisely what the phrase means. A dogmatic conclusion is impossible. What we all agree on is that the image of God is what sets men apart from other creations of God. Today we refer to what is distinct about man by using the word "personal." Man is personal; other animals are not. So we shall use the word "personal" as a synonym for the phrase "the image of God." This is especially helpful to us if we remember that we have already used the word "personal" to describe God. God is personal, and man is personal, which means that he is made in the image of God.

It is unnecessary to define what is meant by the word "personal." A definition consists of words which point to a more immediate experience than the word they are to define. But no experience is more immediate to us than the experience of being persons. In other words, we do not need to define "personal" because we *are* personal. Therefore we know what it is to be created in God's image.

What we can do is to select some aspects of our personal life for special attention. Two of these to which I want to call your attention are our experience of freedom and our experience of society.

Men have freedom to make decisions. This is presupposed in the Genesis story of the Garden of Eden where man is forbidden to eat fruit from a certain tree, and it is taken for granted throughout the Bible in all the stories in which men are held accountable for their actions. I believe that freedom is a gift given by the creator to his creation. God wants us to make decisions.

There are limitations to our choices, of course. We cannot choose to do some things (like jump over a building) or to believe some things (that I am the only person who speaks English). So our freedom is always within limits. But it is real freedom, nevertheless. You do not have to have complete freedom in order to have real freedom. If in the course of a day you make one real decision then you have experienced freedom. Your freedom is partial but it is real.

Men are responsible for the decisions they make. They are to be commended for good decisions, and they are guilty for bad decisions. If they did not have freedom, then they would not be responsible for their actions. We do not call computers good or bad for their activities, since they are all programmed. Responsibility comes with freedom.

Sometimes it is difficult to know if a person has acted in freedom or if he has been programmed so that he is not responsible for his actions. Judges are often called upon to decide in certain situations whether a man is legally responsible for an act or whether he was mentally incompetent and so not responsible for what he did. Parents also have to decide whether an action of a child is simply programmed and inevitable or whether the child is really responsible for what he did. These judgments are sometimes hard to make, and each situation must be considered individually. The fact is, though, that we do make these judgments, which is a recognition that freedom exists in some instances.

Freedom is a frightening thing, and many people seek to evade it. Although men talk as if they want freedom, in reality they usually don't. They do not want to be held accountable for their actions. But freedom is a reality of personal life and cannot be evaded. God has made us this way; he is thrusting decisions on us just as he did on Adam and Eve. Our evasion of freedom is an indication of how far away we have come from God's purposes for us.

Some people do not agree with what I am saying; they feel that belief in God stifles human freedom. It is true that some views of God are incompatible with freedom. For example, if God has determined in advance every "decision" of man, then men would not really be free at all. This idea is sometimes called predestination, but it would be better to call it fatalism. All that it is really necessary to affirm in order to be loyal to the biblical teaching about predestination is that *in the end* God will achieve his purposes. It is not necessary to affirm that God pre-determines every choice of man. We shall speak later on of the purposes of God, and then we shall see that they are not only compatible with man's freedom but they require it. So when we say that we believe in God, we are not denying man's freedom. We are in fact affirming the foundation upon which human freedom rests, for it is God who makes men free.

Some thinkers believe that freedom is an illusion. It is true that sometimes when we feel that we are acting freely we really are not. Our decisions are sometimes determined by forces we are not aware of. But there is no reason to think that this is always so.

More recently, thinkers have held that freedom is really not a good thing. The Harvard psychologist B. F. Skinner, in his book *Beyond Freedom and Dignity*, said that American society should give up its belief that freedom is a virtue. We should program our people so that we can do away with evils like racism, war, ignorance, greed, and so on. I do not doubt the ability of behavioral psychologists to program people so that the people lose their freedom. Perhaps they could even manage to create a society without some of the horrible evils we see in our world today. Their power to control men's minds is not in question.

What is in question is the wisdom of doing so. The

difficulty with freedom is that people may make choices which we had rather they did not make. Parents who want their child to make his own decisions may find that the child decides to rebel against his parents. It is when freedom is misused that we are compelled to decide whether we *really* want people to be free. Do we really believe in freedom? Why should we, if a happier world could be created simply by taking away men's freedom?

The story in Genesis of the creation of man is the story of God giving man freedom even to rebel. I believe that freedom is so important that God chose to give it to us even though we could use it to reject him. My feeling is that it is only here—on the foundation of God's creation of free men—that we may rest the case for the worthwhileness of freedom. I do not know of any other foundation for freedom that can withstand the radical criticism of freedom which we encounter in Professor Skinner's book. Because I believe that God made us free even to rebel against him, I also believe in the worthwhileness of freedom even when it is put to bad uses.

In describing the experiences of personal life we have described men as free. To this we now add that men are social. By "social" I mean that personal life includes relationships with other persons. God made us to live in these relationships. In the creation story in Genesis God says: "It is not good for the man to be alone. I will provide a partner for him" (Genesis 1:18). So God created the first society, Adam and Eve.

We need other people if we are to be persons ourselves. In the Tarzan stories an infant was raised by apes and became a man, but I do not think that this would really happen. A child raised by apes would be an ape, more or less. He would not think like a person, or feel like a person, or speak like a person, or behave like a person. If later on in life he lived with people, he might become a person, but he could not live a personal life apart from other persons. We need society to be personal.

In the past some Christians have felt that society was evil

and that individual men are good, but this is not exactly true. It is true that men are influenced for evil by society; it is also true that they are influenced for good by society. Society is just other people, and they may influence us either way. But it is wrong to say that a hermit is a better person for being alone.

Nor is our freedom always lessened when we live in relationships with other people. Sometimes our relationships do limit our freedom, but sometimes freedom is heightened by social relationships, as when a teacher enlarges the horizons of a student so that he has more options for his life than he would otherwise have had. Even when becoming involved with other people means the sacrifice of some of our freedoms, this is not necessarily bad. This involvement is a choice in itself, and in turn it may open up possibilities of freedom of other kinds.

In any case, society is necessary if we are to be persons, so our initial possibilities of freedom depend upon others. If it is true that sometimes we lose ourselves in society, it is also true that we can never find ourselves without society. The point that I wish to make here is that our social experiences are part of what it means to be personal, and so they are part of what it means to be created in God's image.

Let us summarize what we have said about man thus far. We have said that men are creations of God. This is as true of you and me as it is of Adam and Eve. It is a good thing to be a creation of God. Since we are creations we recognize that there are limits to our lives. We are like others of God's creations, especially animals, but we are also unique. God created us to be personal, which means that we have limited but real freedom and that we have relationships with other people.

So far everything that we have said about ourselves has been good. Being a creation, being like animals, being personal, having freedom and social relations, even being finite—all these are good. Now we turn to the dark side of human life.

Men Are Sinners Before God

There is a positive relationship between God and man: men are creations of God. There is also a negative relationship between God and man: men are sinners before God. Because men stand in these two relationships before God, human life is filled with contradictions and ambiguities. Persons are good, but something has gone wrong with that goodness. Human life is characterized by grandeur and by tragedy. From a single person we hear truth and lies. In one world we find peacelovers and warmongers.

Everyone today agrees that our world is in serious trouble, and most individuals seem to feel that the same thing is true about their personal lives. The human problem has been diagnosed in various ways. It is said that our technology dehumanizes us, or that unequal distribution of wealth leads to class strife, or that poor education results in ignorance, or that our emotions either cause us anxiety if we repress them or produce destructive behavior if we allow them to erupt. All these analyses see our predicament in terms of certain relationships: to machines, to money, to education, or to our emotions. To these the Christian adds that men are in a negative relationship with God. They are sinners.

There are two parts to our predicament before God. One part is that we use our freedom to make choices that are contrary to God's purposes. We will call this part of the predicament, somewhat arbitrarily, our *sins*. The other part of the human predicament does not arise from any identifiable human decision. It consists of the problems that are built into our disposition or into nature or into the structures of our world. No one seems to be responsible, but things are still in terrible shape. We will call this part of the predicament, also somewhat arbitrarily, our *sin*. Both of these parts of our predicament before God must be acknowledged if we are to recognize the entire problem. If we acknowledge only one part then we will have a wrong view of our predicament.

Let us begin with the sins that we commit. The classic

example of this is from the story of the Garden of Eden. Adam and Eve were forbidden by God to eat a certain fruit; they ate it, which was disobedience.

We are all familiar with disobedience like this. Children play with forbidden matches, youngsters smoke marijuana, adults cheat on their income tax, husbands are unfaithful to their wives, employees steal from their employers, politicians deceive their constituencies, people of one color despise people of another color, strong nations behave treacherously toward weak nations. There is little doubt that much of our predicament is due to our freedom to make choices. We choose to act in ways that violate standards we know are good, and so we make a mess of our lives and our world. Not all our choices are bad, of course. We do some good things. But some of our choices are wrong, and that is part of our human problem.

One of the great forces that shaped American Protestantism into what it is today is the movement called revivalism which began with John Wesley. One characteristic of revivalistic preaching is its stress upon individual responsibility. That preaching calls our attention to the fact that we do bad things. And so it should, for we do commit sins. Choosing to do wrong is part of our problem.

But there is another part too. Some of our problem is not of our own choice. Diseases are not, nor are earthquakes and floods. Sometimes, even when our intentions are good, our actions bring disaster. Sometimes we try to do good and we are unable; some force compels us to do bad. Sometimes we are really blind to what is good, and in our blindness we do wrong. Sometimes we can see the good but do not have the energy to do it. Almost everyone today professes to love peace, but no one seems to be able to stop wars. We are all against poverty, but there seems to be no way to prevent all of it. We all want to put an end to race and class hatred, but as soon as we put it down in one place it appears in another place. Ironically, many of our efforts to do right produce results which are as bad as the problem. Our cures are sometimes worse than our diseases.

The Bible gives us analyses of both parts of our problem. There are lists of our sins in Romans 1-3 and elsewhere; we deceive, steal, fornicate, and so on. And in Romans 5-7 the sin problem is described as an inner principle.

> I am unspiritual, the purchased slave of sin. I do not even acknowledge my own actions as mine, for what I do is not what I want to do, but what I detest...But as things are, it is no longer I who perform the action, but sin that lodges in me. (Romans 7:14-17)

In Ephesians the sin problem is analyzed not only in terms of an individual but in terms of the entire world.

> Time was when you were dead in your sins and wickedness, when you followed the evil ways of this present age, when you obeyed the commander of the spiritual powers of the air, the spirit now at work among God's rebel subjects. (Ephesians 2:1-2)

In this passage our problem includes our doing wrong ("sins"); but it includes also an inner helplessness ("dead"), an environment we cannot escape ("this present age"), and demonic forces that control us ("the commander of the spiritual powers of the air"). This is the traditional analysis of the sin problem in terms of the world, the flesh, and the devil. These three factors are probably three descriptions of the same reality. All are names for the oppressive forces which destroy our lives, enslave us, and separate us from God.

It is a traditional Christian teaching that men are born with the sin problem. This offends many people. They point out that no infant can be responsible for his actions. This is quite true. The point of the traditional Christian teaching is simply that we do not begin our lives in neutral. We begin in a corrupt world, not in a Garden of Eden. We begin with problems whose potential will develop as time goes on. Certainly no child is guilty of committing sins, but he does begin his life with the predicament called the world-flesh-devil.

Christians are not naive about the seriousness of the man's problem. The human problem does not begin at some hypothetical "age of accountability" at which an innocent child suddenly becomes a furious rebel against God. Freedom comes to a growing child intermittently. He begins to make selfish choices and to act in irresponsible ways, but these acts are only the outward visible part of an inward invisible problem. Culpable as he is for them—and it would be wrong to underestimate his guilt—still the problem began long before he acted; it permeates the world, and no one can escape it.

The Baptist Faith and Message recognizes that the human predicament has two parts. It says that "by his free choice man sinned against God," and it also alludes to our heritage as "a nature and an environment inclined towards sin." The words "inclined toward sin" testify to the fact that the human problem is too big for us. To be bad we have only to coast downhill; to be good we must struggle uphill; no one ever manages to struggle uphill completely.

If we fail to take the second part of the human predicament seriously, we will not understand how dire the human condition is. To put it bluntly: Mankind cannot free itself from the sin problem. Perhaps we could stamp out poverty—if we were willing to forego freedom. Perhaps we could stop criminal activity—if we were willing to execute all criminals. Perhaps we could educate all people—if we were willing to manipulate and brainwash them. Perhaps we could have democratic governments—if we were willing to tolerate the abuse of minorities by the majority. The structures of our world are somehow set against the simultaneous achievement of all the values we know to be worthwhile. That is why utopian dreams cannot become realities: We cannot achieve one value without jeopardizing or forfeiting another. Life, like politics, is the art of the possible; utopia is not possible. The Christian diagnosis of the human predicament is realistic and grim.

It is not as important to recognize the details of the

problem as it is to recognize the two parts. Some of our problem is our own fault—we do wrong. And some of it is not our fault—things go wrong. For our sins we are guilty and need forgiveness; in our sin we are helpless and need liberation.

These two parts are not entirely separate, of course; there is interaction between them. The sin problem (understood as world or flesh or devil) entices us to commit sins, and the sins we commit contribute to the great sin problem because the consequences of our bad choices move beyond our control. But right now it is enough if we recognize the two parts of the problem.

We said that men are creations of God and sinners before God. Now we want to say that the second relationship does not cancel out the first. Though we are in a terrible mess, we are still God's creations. Even sinners exist by God's creative activity.

But, of course, we are not in a proper relationship to him. God created us for a purpose, and that purpose is not being fulfilled because of our sins and because of sin. The God who creates us is the only one who can save us from our predicament. The creator is the savior.

We have done a better job of communicating to people generally that God is creator than we have that he is savior. If you ask people on the streets what the word "God" means, most will reply in terms of creation: "God is the one who made the world." We need to communicate to them better that God is also the savior. The same God who made us also saves us.

For Christians, the opposite is often necessary. They know God as savior. They need to be reminded that their savior is also the creator. God's purposes are as wide as all of creation.

In salvation we see how deep his purposes are. To those deep purposes we now turn our attention.

For further reading:

The Christian understanding of man becomes clear when it is contrasted with other views, as in Perry LeFevre's *Understandings of Man.* For a traditional Christian statement on man see Sydney Cave, *The Christian Estimate of Man.* Ronald Gregor Smith helpfully treats man as historical in *The Problem of God,* chapter 5. For a good treatment of man in terms of Jesus, see David Jenkins, *The Glory of Man.* Many Christians receive their view of man from non-theological books like Paul Tournier's *The Meaning of Persons,* and then they try to relate this to God.

5. JESUS

Introduction

Our theology is Christian because we believe that in Jesus Christ God reconciled the world to himself. That is the presupposition with which we have been working throughout this book.

Having affirmed that Jesus is the solution to the human predicament, we are now going to turn our attention directly to Jesus himself. When we do this, Jesus becomes a problem as well as a solution for us. To think about him is to raise two sets of questions.

One set concerns his saving work. How did Jesus deal with the human predicament of sins and sin? How did he, by his death and resurrection, provide forgiveness and liberation for us? We shall try to respond to this set of questions in Chapter Six.

The other set of questions concerns Jesus as a person. Who and what was Jesus? What was his relationship to God whom we have described as personal, transcendent, good, and loving? What was his relationship to men who are creations of God and sinners before God? In the words of Jesus to his disciples at Caesarea Philippi: "Who do you say that I am?" (Matthew 16:15). We shall try to respond to these questions in this chapter.

We recognize that these questions are very important, so we find it understandable that the church has put much time and effort into trying to answer them. In fact, more creeds have been formulated, more councils have met, more heresies have been condemned, more books have been written in this struggle to understand Jesus, than in dealing with any other part of Christian teaching. Whether we know it or not, these efforts of the church have shaped the understanding of all of us who live after them. Therefore in this chapter I shall be referring to some of the history of christology (the doctrine about Christ) which is especially important to us today.

Who Was Jesus?

The first Christians were Jewish men and women. They worshiped the God who had delivered Israel out of Egypt at the Exodus. When they came to know Jesus of Nazareth, they believed that he was the deliverer whom they were awaiting, that is, the Messiah or Christ, God's anointed one. This is the meaning of Peter's confession: "Thou are the Christ." But though Peter sensed that Jesus was the expected Christ, he did not realize that Jesus was to save men from sin by death and resurrection. Perhaps he thought that God would bring the world to an end and give Jesus control of everything, or that Jesus would organize an army to drive the Romans out of Israel. In any case, he was not prepared for Jesus to die (see Matthew 16:13-23).

But Jesus did die, and three days later he was raised from the dead and seen by many of his followers. When they saw him alive, they were convinced that he was someone special, more than the greatest of the prophets. The resurrection compelled the disciples to revise their way of understanding Jesus.

As long as Christians were Jewish people, words like "Christ" were adequate for describing Jesus. In his sermon at the festival of Pentecost Peter could say:

> Let all the house of Israel therefore know assuredly that God has made Him both Lord and Christ, this Jesus whom ye crucified (Acts 2:36).

Peter meant that the resurrection of Jesus confirmed that Jesus really was the Christ. From a Jewish point of view, this confession was sufficient.

But as the church began to include non-Jewish persons, the word "Christ" no longer served as a divine title, for the Gentiles did not know what "Christ" meant. The Gentile church stopped using "Christ" as a title and began to use it as a name. Jesus became known as Jesus Christ.

Other titles, like "Lord," were employed by the early church to affirm something similar to "Christ"—that Jesus was more than a prophet. These titles reveal that the church unconsciously associated Jesus with God. A few passages in the New Testament indicate that some early Christians also made a conscious association of Jesus with God. One of these is in Paul's letter to the Philippians:

> Let your bearing towards one another arise out of your life in Christ Jesus. For the divine nature was his from the first; yet he did not think to snatch at equality with God, but made himself nothing, assuming the nature of a slave. Bearing the human likeness, revealed in human shape, he humbled himself, and in obedience accepted even death—death on a cross. Therefore God raised him to the heights and bestowed on him the name above all names, that at the name of Jesus every knee should bow—in heaven, on earth, and in the depths—and every tongue confess, 'Jesus Christ is Lord', to the glory of God the Father. (Philippians 2:5-11)

In encouraging Christians to be humble Paul cited the great humility of Jesus who, though he had "the divine nature," made himself nothing and died on a cross. After this ultimate sacrifice God raised him, and so everyone will be compelled to acknowledge that "Jesus is Lord." This passage, and others like it, show us that the church thought of Christ as existing before his birth. Pre-existence is a metaphor taken from our time reference. It was not intended to jeopardize the teaching that Jesus was really born, that he was really Mary's son. Rather it was intended to affirm that even though Jesus was born he was nevertheless to be identified with God who is eternal.

Another passage which showed a conscious association of Jesus with God is found in Hebrews:

> In many and various ways God spoke of old to our fathers by the prophets; but in these last days he has spoken to us by a Son, whom he appointed the heir of all things, through whom also he created the world.
>
> (Hebrews 1:1-2)

This passage follows a pattern which is often repeated in Hebrews. The writer tells us that Jesus was superior to the prophets, Law, sacrifices, and other aspects of Old Testament religion.

But we notice that the writer also identified Jesus with the creative activity of God. Like pre-existence in Philippians, creation is here used as a way of expressing this writer's association of Jesus of Nazareth with the eternal creator of the universe. It is not intended to jeopardize the teaching that Jesus was himself "made of woman" (Galatians 4:4), and it does not imply that as he lay in his crib he was secretly exercising cosmic functions. Rather it is affirming that though Jesus lay in a crib, he is nevertheless to be identified with the God who creates and orders the universe.

The stories of Jesus' birth to Mary the virgin are also conscious expressions of the church's association of Jesus with God. Both Matthew (1:18) and Luke (1:26-35) tell us that Mary's son was God's son. The virgin birth is an expression, taken from what we all know about how children are conceived, of the fact that Jesus is to be associated with God. It does not mean that he was somehow less than fully human or that he had only half as many chromosomes as other persons. That is not the intention of the writers. Their intention is to say that Jesus is identified with God as his unique son.

A final passage which shows us how one early Christian associated Jesus with God is the prologue to the Gospel of John. In it we read:

> In the beginning was the Word, and the Word was with God, and the Word was God . . . And the Word became flesh and dwelt among us, full of grace and truth; we have beheld his glory, glory as of the only Son from the Father. (John 1:1, 14, RSV)

This passage introduces yet another way of expressing the association of Jesus with God. It describes Jesus as the divine Word (*Logos*) who has become flesh. This does not mean that the Word ceased to be divine and became human—to say that would be to forget the analogical character of this language. What is being expressed here is that Jesus is God in the flesh living with us. It is an expression of (not a solution to) the mysterious but real presence of God with us in Jesus.

These passages contain four different ways of saying the same thing. When they say that Jesus was pre-existent, that he exercised cosmic functions, that his mother was a virgin, and that he was the Word become flesh, the writers are consciously affirming that he was divine. Since these passages represent five different writers (Paul, Matthew, Luke, John, and the author of Hebrews), I think it is reasonable to say that the conscious and unconscious consensus of the early church identified Jesus with God.

But it did so in an indirect manner, for none of these passages uses direct words like "Jesus is God." If the church unconsciously and consciously believed that Jesus was God, why did they not just say it directly? I think there were two reasons. One is that the question was never put to early Christians as directly as it is to us: "Is Jesus God or not?" Since the question was not put that directly, they were not motivated to answer it that directly. The second reason is that affirming Jesus' deity created a problem for Jewish monotheists. This problem did not seem as troublesome when the affirmation was made indirectly as it would have seemed if the affirmations had been direct.

I believe, in other words, that the direction of the New Testament answer to the question "Who is Jesus?" is clearly "He is God." But in the New Testament the confession is not yet made so directly. Later on, when the church was confronted directly with the question of Christ's deity, then the church answered directly and so was directly forced to cope with the problems which that answer raises.

A variety of affirmations about the divinity of Jesus was made during the second and third centuries. Finally, in the fourth century, the direct question about Jesus' deity was asked by Arius, a minister in Alexandria, Egypt. Recognizing that many of the phrases which Christians used about Jesus were ambiguous, he decided to clear up the uncertainties. He pointed out that there are only two kinds of reality: There is the creator, and there is everything else. He felt that the church had hesitated long enough about Jesus. As for himself, he had made a decision: Jesus was a creature, not God. He was a great, good, eminently important creature, but he was not God.

Arius soon met opposition from Athanasius, another Alexandrian, who rejected the idea that Jesus was merely a creature. This young man had written a book describing Jesus as the incarnation of the Word (*Logos*) of God. He argued that since Jesus saves us, he must be God. In this connection he wrote:

> There were thus two things which the Saviour did for us by becoming man. He banished death from us and made us anew; and, invisible and imperceptible as in Himself He is, He became visible through His works and revealed Himself as the Word of the Father, the Ruler and King of the whole creation.[1]

The debate between Arians and other Christians became so furious that Constantine, who was the first pro-Christian Roman emperor, called a large council of church leaders to reconcile the warring parties. In 325 A.D. they met in a town named Nicea and condemned the teaching of Arius. In a rather daring move they adopted a word which was not biblical to describe Jesus as divine. They said he was "of one substance" (*homo-ousios*) with the Father. This outraged the

[1] Athanasius, *The Incarnation of the Word of God*, section 16.

Arians who wanted to say no more than that Jesus was "of similar substance" (*homoi-ousios*) to the Father.

The statement made by the Council of Nicea was the first official ecumenical (worldwide) church pronouncement about Jesus. In the 1600 years since then, the church has over and over again repeated this conviction: Jesus is God. For example, when the World Council of Churches met in New Delhi in 1961, they confessed "the Lord Jesus Christ as God and Saviour." That phrase sounds like it came right out of the fourth century. As a Baptist I am not required to believe the teachings of church councils, but I agree with what was said at Nicea. I am glad that from Nicea onward it became natural for Christians to respond to the question, "Who was Jesus?" with the answer, "He was God."

What Was Jesus?

For those of us who are the heirs of the affirmations of the Bible and of the struggles of the fourth century, it is relatively simple to state who Jesus was, since we have only to identify him as the God whom we described in Chapter Three as transcendent, personal, good, and loving. Likewise, it is relatively simple to say what he was, since we have only to say that he was a man, and in Chapter Four we described what it is to be a man.

In the New Testament Jesus is described as a real man. He is born and dies, he works and suffers, he travels and speaks, he experiences joy and sadness, he has friends and enemies. It is an assumption of writers of the New Testament that Jesus was a man like other men.

The earliest error concerning Christ about which we read in the Bible concerned his true humanity. It was known as docetism (*dokein* means "to appear") because it said that Jesus did not have a real body; he only appeared to have a body. This view was held by people with good intentions who believed that physical things were bad and that the Spirit was good. They reasoned that God who is pure spirit can have no real relationship to a physical body. They denied, therefore, that the divine Christ was a human being. We find this view challenged in several passages in the New Testament. For example:

> But do not trust any and every Spirit, my friends; test the Spirits to see whether they are from God, for among those who have gone out into the world are many prophets falsely inspired. This is how we may recognize the Spirit of God: every Spirit which acknowledges that Jesus Christ has come *in the flesh* is from God, and every Spirit which does not thus acknowledge Jesus is not from God. (I John 4:1-3)

So, according to the New Testament, Jesus was a man, one of the group of God's creations who are personal human beings. This is always assumed, occasionally expressed in various descriptions, and specifically defended in opposition to docetism.

As a man the characteristics which we discussed in Chapter Four apply to Christ, with one exception. Let us examine these characteristics. First, he is described as created (Colossians 1:15). Perhaps no one word makes clearer the mystery of Christ than the word "created." How can he be both the creator and created? That is the paradox about him in a very few words.

Second, as a creation he was both good and finite. That he was good is no problem to us. But we have real difficulty with the word finite. Nevertheless, the New Testament speaks of the reality of his body (which was finite), of his growth in wisdom, stature, and favor with God and men (Luke 2:52), of his not knowing the time of his own return (Matthew 24:36), of the limits of his physical strength, of his reaction to pain. All of these are witnesses to the fact that he lived within the kind of limitations which are common to all men. In other words, he was finite.

As personal, he was free and social. His freedom is apparent in that he chose his disciples, he made decisions about his ministry, and he wrestled with temptations. Socially, the importance of his Jewish heritage is apparent in his teachings, and he was involved in the life of the Jewish people. We know something of his family. We see him call disciples, and later he asks three of them to watch while he prays. We see him in relationships with a variety of people.

Finally, men are characterized by their predicament of sins and sin. Jesus committed no sins. We sometimes describe that as his sinlessness, though a negative word does not do justice to his moral achievement. He did not simply avoid breaking rules. Rather, he loved his Father with all his heart, mind, soul, and strength, and he loved his neighbor as himself, even to the point of laying down his life for his friends. He sought God's kingdom first. He obeyed his Father's will.

Although he did not commit any sins, Jesus did participate in the human predicament of sin. He experienced temptation to sins. He felt the power of the devil and the influence of the world. I am not sure what his experience of "the flesh," was like. In Romans we read that "God sent His Son in the likeness of sinful flesh" (Romans 8:3). In any case, if world, flesh, devil, and so on, are all descriptions of a single reality—that part of man's predicament for which he is not responsible—then I believe we can say that Jesus experienced the sin problem, though, of course, he was not enslaved by it as other men are. Finally, in fact, he destroyed it.

So Jesus was fully human, except that he was good and all other men are sinners. One of the most serious challenges to the true humanity of Jesus came in the fourth century. From the time of Arius on, the church was busy defending the deity of Jesus. One seemingly innocent way to defend his deity was to minimize his humanity; that finally happened about 380 A.D.

One of the most ardent supporters of Christ's deity was an educator named Apollinarius. He believed that to be a man is to have a body, a life-force (soul), and a mind. Apollinarius said that Jesus had a human body like other men and a human life-force like other men. But instead of a human mind, Jesus had the Word (Reason) of God, and that is the sense in which he was God.

This position was quickly challenged by other theologians. The Archbishop of Constantinople pointed out that if Jesus did not have a human mind, then he was not really human, however real his body may have been. He wrote:

> If anyone has put his trust in Jesus as a man without a human mind, *he* is really bereft of mind, and quite unworthy of salvation. For that which Jesus has not assumed he has not healed; but that which is united to his Godhead is also saved. (Gregory of Nazianzus, Epistle 101).

I believe that Gregory is correct. Jesus' mind was fully human as his body was. The New Testament bears witness to this in passages which I mentioned above.

In my judgment, if there is a danger among evangelical Christians today of rejecting the accepted teaching about Jesus, it is here. For example, we often notice a tendency to deny that Jesus was really limited in his knowledge. His knowledge, more than anything else, is a problem to twentieth century Christians. The motive behind this denial is very good; it is the desire to affirm the full deity of Jesus. But that good motive pushes us into a poor position when we find ourselves refusing to admit that what the New Testament plainly says is true, that Jesus increased in wisdom (Luke 2:52).

A second way in which we fail to accept the reality of Jesus' humanity is in our attempts to reason about what Jesus "must have been" like. You cannot use logic alone to learn what a person in history was like. To learn about a person you must know him or else depend on the records of those who knew him. But we continue to reason about Jesus, thus subtly denying his real and historical humanity. It is wrong to argue, for example: "God is omniscient; Jesus was God; therefore Jesus was omniscient." This is logical, but it does not take account of the fact that Jesus was a real man with human limitations. We see the error in this logic in the following examples:

> "God has no parents; Jesus was God; therefore Jesus had no parents."

"God cannot be tempted; Jesus was God; therefore Jesus was not tempted."

"God cannot die; Jesus was God; therefore Jesus did not die."

In each case the logic is correct, but the conclusions are all wrong. To learn what Jesus was like, we must turn to the Bible. There we learn that Mary was his mother, that he was tempted, and that he died. Then we realize that, though he was God, he was God living under the circumstances of a human life. We must not jeopardize the reality of those human circumstances by employing a logic which could lead us to contradict the witness of the Bible.

A third challenge to the reality of Jesus' humanity takes the form of affirming that he was the perfect man. It is true that Jesus was good and we are sinners, so he was the real man and we are imperfect men. But we must not allow his humanity in the sense of his moral achievement to eclipse the reality of the human condition which he accepted, including its limitations.

All three of these challenges to Jesus' humanity are made with the best intentions. They arise because we want to emphasize that he was God. But they mistakenly suppose that by denying his humanity they can emphasize his deity. Clearly this will not do. Both his deity and his humanity must be affirmed.

This brings us, then to our next problem: How did God become a man?

Jesus, who was conceived of the Holy Spirit and born of the virgin Mary, was both divine and human. Both his conception and his birth affirm that he was divine and human, but neither one explains how it happened, as you can see if you ask the further question: How then did this conception and birth unite the divine and human?

The virgin birth of Christ is a great mystery, but it is not what we usually take it to mean. It is certainly more important than a case of parthenogenesis (birth by one parent) which a geneticist might investigate. And its importance does not consist of its explaining how Jesus could be God and man, for it does not explain that. What is really remarkable, from the point of view of a person who believes that Jesus was divine, is not that Jesus had no human father; what really stuns us is that he did have a human mother! This is the unexpected, the startling, the miraculous, that a woman should bear a child who was God.

Over the centuries the church has used many verbs to describe the activity which resulted in the existence of the one who was divine and human. Here are a few of them.

God *came* into the world.
God *took* human nature.
God *humbled* himself to the human condition.
God *united* human nature to himself.
God *used* a human nature.
God *became* a man.

Because the church uses these expressions, the impression is created that we have some idea of how the great event occurred. We do not. Like all words which are used of God, these are analogies, and they should not be taken literally. We can see how wrong this would be by asking questions like: Did he *come* into the world on a rocket ship? When he *used* human nature did it wear out? When he *became* a man did he cease to be God? These words are not to be taken literally.

But we must take them very seriously. For one thing, all of them indicate that the initiative lies with God, not man, and this is important. The verb "came," which implies distance traversed, indicates how great a deed this was. The verb "humbled" shows the moral and sacrificial qualities of this act. The verb "became" speaks of how by this act God was putting himself into a passive position, that is, was not only acting on earth but also was being acted upon on earth. So when we examine these verbs we find that they give us real help in understanding Jesus. What they cannot do is to tell us precisely how the Word became flesh.

What is the Relation of the Divine and the Human in Christ?

When we admit that we cannot understand the act by which the Word became flesh, then we must try to understand the relationship between the divine and the human in Jesus. In early church history two proposals were made along these lines.

One came from an Archbishop of Constantinople named Nestorius. He reacted strongly against the view of Apollinarius that Jesus did not have a human mind. He said firmly that Jesus was fully human and fully divine. He liked to use a word for their relationship which sounded a little like a word for marriage, *synergia*. It is usually translated as "union."

Nestorius got into trouble because some people felt that the "union" he spoke of wasn't really very strong. (We know now that they probably were wrong, but that wasn't known in the fifth century). Christians in Constantinople were accustomed to call Mary, Jesus' mother, *theotokos*, which meant "bearer of God." Nestorius did not support the use of this word, and so he seemed to be saying that Mary bore the humanity but not the deity of Jesus. The church could not accept this. They were convinced that Jesus was one person, truly divine and human but in no way divided. So the child born of Mary was not just human, he was divine, and it was wrong of Nestorius to divide Jesus in this way.

I fully agree. And I fear that today we sometimes tend to divide Jesus in a Nestorian fashion. We tend to say things like this: "As a man Jesus taught; as God he did miracles." If this means "My attention was called to his deity by his resurrection," then it is correct. But if it means that "He was human in his death but divine in his resurrection," then it is the Nestorian error of dividing Christ into two persons.

The same is true of the paradoxical way of speaking about Jesus. "Christ was both mortal (as man) and immortal (as God)." If this simply points up the great mystery of Christ then it is acceptable, but if it means that he who died on the cross was not God, then it is Nestorian and false. Perhaps we should put the paradoxes even stronger: The Christ who died was God (as well as man), the Christ who was raised was man (as well as God). Used in this unexpected way, the paradoxes speak not only of the very great mystery of his two natures but also simultaneously of the mystery of his unity, and that is an improvement over some of our expressions.

The second proposal in the early church for understanding the relation of the divinity and humanity of Christ came from an elderly priest in Constantinople named Eutyches. His motive was to insist, against Nestorianism, that Christ was really one person. He seems to have thought that the union was possible because of an alteration in both the deity and the humanity of Christ. He was so concerned to say "one person" that he did not care if it involved the implication that Jesus was not *fully* God or *fully* man.

This too is a popular error today; in fact it often poses as the traditional view. I have heard it said that the orthodox view is that Jesus was half God and half man! But that is just what the orthodox theologians rejected when they condemned the teachings of Eutyches at the Fourth Ecumenical Council (Chalcedon) in 451 A.D. Here is part of their famous statement:

> We all teach harmoniously that Jesus is
> perfect in Godhead
> perfect in manhood. . . .
> without change,
> without division.

Against Arius the church affirmed that Jesus was truly God and against Apollinarius that He was truly man. Against Eutyches it affirmed that Jesus' deity and humanity were not changed into something else, and against Nestorius that Jesus was not divided into two persons. Though the statement of Chalcedon is couched in very technical language, and though it deals with matters beyond the scope of the New Testament, I believe that it is compatible with the teaching of the New

Testament and that it is true.

Now let us turn our attention to the efforts of some modern theologians who have tried to speak meaningfully of Jesus. Some of the impetus for these efforts has come from a vigorous study of the New Testament, trying to interpret it without seeing it through the eyes of the bishops at Chalcedon. Modern biblical scholars have introduced a technical distinction between a functional and an ontological christology. By a functional christology they mean that God acted in Christ to save the world; Christ functioned as God. Now this certainly is true, and it is a biblical way of speaking as we can see by reading II Corinthians 5:19. By an ontological christology they mean any christology which employs philosophical concepts like "nature" or "essence" which were used at Chalcedon; Christ in his essence was God. Many of the New Testament scholars do not find any ontological christology in the New Testament. Speaking of the New Testament, one of them has written: "Functional christology is the only kind which exists."[1] The functional christologies are probably the most widely accepted ones in the twentieth century.

I want to make two comments about functional christologies. First, the fact that the New Testament did not use ontological terms (if it is indeed a fact) does not mean that it is wrong for us to use them. Neither did the New Testament writers make a distinction between ontological and functional concepts and then select the functional ones, which is what the scholar quoted above has done. We cannot always be true to the teaching of the New Testament simply by following its terminologies. There are times when, to convey its meaning to people in our time, we must use terms which are not found in the New Testament.

Second, it is in any case unnecessary to use ontological terms to try to state what is omitted in the functional christologies. The strength of the functional christologies is that they tell us that God was active in Christ; their

[1]Oscar Cullman, *The Christology of the New Testament*, p. 326.

weakness is that they fail to tell us whether God was passive in Christ. In my mind there is no question but that the early Christians, and those at Chalcedon too, felt that in Christ God was acted upon by the world as well as that God acted upon the world.

Theologians of the Reformation used to speak of the active and passive obedience of Christ in his passion. He obeyed the Father's command, and he also accepted the sufferings which were inflicted by his persecutors. I shall speak in the next chapter of this active and passive obedience, but right now I want to call attention to the fact that in Christ God was both acting and being acted upon. The Christ who accepted the limitations of a human historical existence and the outrages of vicious people was divine. God was experiencing firsthand the cruelty of men.

In my judgment, if we can affirm this then we can affirm what was intended at Chalcedon. It is not necessary to use philosophical language about "two natures." Men in our century are concerned to know whether God has really become so identified with us that he knows what it is like to suffer. I believe that he does. I think that idea was already under way when Matthew applied to Jesus the name "Emmanuel," God with us.

A second way of understanding Jesus in the twentieth century is called "kenotic christology." The name came from a word in Philippians 2:8 which might be understood as "he limited himself." Because this christology was given this name, it was often thought to have been an attempt to explain *how* Jesus came to be what he was (by imposing limits on himself). But this was not the intention of theologians like Charles Gore, P. T. Forsyth, and H. R. Mackintosh who held this view. Rather they felt that they were simply affirming consistently the fact of Jesus' deity and the fact of his humanity which, they believed, involved limitations. The importance of the kenotic christologies resides, I think, in their intention to take all of Jesus' human limitations with full seriousness and in their conviction that in so doing they did not in any way jeopardize the reality of his deity. Prior to the kenotic christologies no one who believed that Jesus was divine had spoken so frankly, even happily, about Jesus' limitations, especially about the limitations of his knowledge. I believe that we who confess Jesus' full humanity are indebted to the kenotic christologies for showing us that in so doing we have not jeopardized his deity.

A third way of expressing the truth about Jesus is to say that he is the revelation of God to us. This is put in a wonderful way by J. B. Phillips:

> Any attempt by the ordinary man to "imagine" God results in nothing but the "vague oblong blur" complained of by those modern people who make the attempt. Yet if a man can see God focused and be convinced that he is seeing God, scaled-down but authentic, he can . . . add all the other inklings and impressions that he has of the majesty, magnificence, and order of the Infinite Being, and "see God." . . .
>
> It is a fascinating problem for us human beings to consider how the Eternal Being—wishing to show men His own Character focused, His own Thought expressed, and His own Purpose demonstrated—could introduce Himself into the stream of human history without disturbing or disrupting it. There must obviously be an almost unbelievable "scaling-down" of the "size" of God to match the life of the planet. There must be a complete acceptance of the space-and-time limitations of this present life. The thing must be done properly—it must not, for example, be merely an act put on for man's benefit. If it is to be done at all God must *be* man.[1]

Phillips was saying that Jesus was God in focus for us. You can see the need for such a focus if you ask yourself: "How *could* God best show himself to us so that we could know him?" Whatever we may say about the means of revelation we have spoken of (nature, history, and the Bible), none could be as effective as God being with us. And that is why Jesus was the supreme revelation of God, for he was God with us.

[1]J. B. Phillips, *Your God is Too Small*, pp. 72-73.

Another theologian has tried to wrestle with the question to which Eutyches succumbed, namely: "If Jesus was one person, how could he have been fully divine and fully human?" Donald M. Baille observed that in our Christian experience there is a "paradox of grace." While we may sometimes think that God is most active when we are passive, and that God is forced to be passive when we actively take charge of our lives, this is not true. The truth is that the more fully we are in control of our lives, making the right choices and so on, the more fully God is able to work through us. Clearly this is a paradox, but it is the experience of many Christians. Baillie felt that the same paradox was at work in Jesus. He wrote:

> What I wish to suggest is that this paradox of grace points the way more clearly and makes a better approach than anything else in our experience to the mystery of the Incarnation itself; that this paradox in its fragmentary form in our own Christian lives is a reflection of that perfect union of God and man in the Incarnation on which our whole Christian life depends, and may therefore be our best clue to the understanding of it. In the New Testament we see the man in whom God was incarnate surpassing all other men in refusing to claim anything for Himself independently and ascribing all the goodness to God. We see Him also desiring to take up other men into His own close union with God, that they might be as He was. And if these men, entering in some small measure through Him into that union, experience the paradox of grace for themselves in fragmentary ways, and are constrained to say, 'It was not I but God', may not this be a clue to the understanding of that perfect life in which the paradox is complete and absolute, that life of Jesus which, being the perfection of humanity, is also, and even in a deeper and prior sense, very life of God Himself? If the paradox is a reality in our poor imperfect lives at all, so far as there is any good in them, does not the same or a similar paradox, taken at the perfect and absolute pitch, appear as the mystery of the Incarnation? [1]

[1] D. M. Baillie, *God Was in Christ*, pp. 117-118.

In many ways the analogy which Baillie draws is not ideal. But on the single point of the possibility of a union of full humanity with full deity, it is quite accurate and, I think, helps us to appreciate the reality of this union.

Finally, another recent theologian who has given us some guidance in speaking about Jesus in a meaningful way today was Leonard Hodgson, who wrestled with the question of Jesus in several of his books. One suggestion that he began making as early as 1928 was that we should think of a man as "the self-conscious subject of the experiences of a body in this world of space and time." He did not just mean that men *happen* to have experiences which are mediated through their bodies; he meant that men *are* neither more nor less than the subject of such experiences. If we bear this in mind then we shall be able to feel the force of a story which Hodgson told in one of his last books.

> I can perhaps best present the Christian doctrine by inventing a dialogue between Satan and God after the manner of the book of Job. In this Satan says to God, 'You may call yourself almighty, but there is at least one thing you cannot do, and that is to know from the inside what it means to live as a man, to think, feel and will as one of those creatures of yours, the content of whose minds is given to them by the experiences that come to each of them through being born of a woman at a particular time and place in the history of that world of yours." There is no need to invent a speech for God's reply. It was given in deeds rather than words. In the person of Jesus Christ he was born of Mary, lay as a babe unconscious in his mother's arms, and grew in the knowledge of himself as child, as boy, as man and as Messiah.
>
> This is, in essence, the Christian belief about Christ. If it be true, there is inevitable mystery which gives rise to what is commonly called the christological problem. No more than Satan in my fable can we understand how God could exercise his omniscient almightiness by entering into the experiences of life as a man. All we can say is that the more we ponder over the evidence concerning that earthly life the more we are driven to the conclusion that we can

> give no satisfactory account of it short of recognizing the life as the life of God incarnate.[1]

I do not know of anyone who has wrestled with understanding Jesus more fully than Hodgson, or of anyone who has taken what I understand to be the biblical and traditional view more seriously than he, or of any statement that is more meaningful in our language than this one is, and so I leave it as the final one in this chapter.

I conclude with one observation, that the more deeply we ponder Jesus with our minds and the more fully we appreciate the traditional teaching, the more we are driven to see that the real challenge of Jesus is to our faith rather than to our minds alone. Whatever we understand of him will be minimal; what really matters is whether we respond to him as a person. Can we believe that God cared so much "for us men and for our salvation" that "he was made flesh and dwelt among us?" It is a tremendous claim; it is also a wonderful one.

For further reading:

The article on "God the Son" in *The Baptist Faith and Message* is the least adequate statement in that document, in my judgment. Generally speaking, Catholics have done a better job of presenting the Incarnation than Protestants, and Protestants have done better work on the atonement than Catholics. I expect that this is because there is a heritage on the Incarnation that must be given attention, and there is no authorized heritage on the atonement. I do not know of a really good statement by a Baptist theologian. Of course, there may be one that I am not aware of.

The best survey of this doctrine is the article "Christology" by George S. Hendry in Alan Richardson, ed., *A Dictionary of Christian Theology*. The best analysis I've read of the study of the lives is found in Etienne Trocme, *Jesus as Seen by His Contemporaries*.

[1]Leonard Hodgson, *The Bible and the Training of the Clergy*, p. 55.

The books which do a good job of affirming the deity of Christ and yet take his human limitations seriously are those of the English kenoticists. Among them the best is Charles Gore, *The Incarnation of the Son of God* (1891), though reference may be made to P. T. Forsyth, *The Person and Place of Jesus Christ* (1909) and H. R. Mackintosh, *The Person of Jesus Christ* (1912).

For the documents from the early fathers and councils see E. R. Hardy, ed., *Christology of the Later Fathers*. A good short study of the debates is J.W.C. Wand's *The Four Great Heresies*. The most thorough single-volume study I know of is by A. J. Grillmeier, S.J., *Christ in Christian Tradition*.

For modern statements see Baillie's *God Was in Christ*, Hodgson's *For Faith and Freedom, Volume II*, J. M. Creed, *The Divinity of Jesus Christ*, and Wolfhart Pannenberg, *Jesus: God and Man*.

6. ATONEMENT

Unlike the doctrine of the person of Christ, the doctrine of the atoning work of Christ has never received an authoritative definition in the church. The history of the doctrine is the story of a series of attempts by individual thinkers to express the meaning of Christ's suffering, death, and resurrection. All Christians believe that Christ's death is important, for that is part of the Gospel. But it has been left to individual Christians to try to understand the meaning of his death.

In the New Testament there are various ways to express what Christ achieved by his death. Sometimes it is thought of as a sacrifice offered to God, like the animal sacrifices of the Old Testament (see Hebrews 8-9). Sometimes it is seen as the making of a new covenant between God and man. Closely related to this is the idea that by his death Christ reconciled man to God (see II Corinthians 5). It is said that by his sacrifice Christ justified sinners; justification, a metaphor taken from a court of law, refers to the act of a judge who pronounces a man "Not guilty" (see Romans 3:23-28). In other passages Christ is said to have provided a ransom, the price needed to buy a slave, to secure man's release from bondage to sin and death (see Mark 10:45).

These metaphors show us some of the variety of New Testament interpretations of the atonement. This variety makes it clear that no one way of expressing Christ's achievement is adequate. But neither is it satisfactory simply to list all of these interpretations, for in theology we need to do more than learn a list; we need to think about what the metaphors mean. We must attempt to put them together in some way.

Over the centuries attempts to put together the meaning of atonement have followed one of two general patterns. One pattern is called objective because it teaches that Jesus achieved something once and for all; he performed a finished task. Something was settled, something done, when he cried out "It is finished" (John 19:30). One theologian (Anselm) said that Jesus made satisfaction to the honor of God for the sins of men. Another (Calvin) said that Jesus accepted the penalty which was due to men for their wrongdoing. The objective pattern, which receives support from several of the biblical metaphors, is usually considered the conservative view.

Other theologians developed views of the atonement which did not fit into the objective pattern. Known as subjective, these views insist that the cross was the beginning, not the end, of God's saving work. What Christ did was to give his life so unselfishly and sacrificially that men are moved very deeply to follow him as their Guide and Master. We are touched by his love, and so we are transformed. The subjective pattern, which also can find support in the Bible, is usually considered the liberal view.

Some of the debates between proponents of these two views have been acrimonious. For this reason, and also because it is difficult to unite the New Testament materials into a single perspective, many Christians avoid the subject of the atonement altogether. One friend of mine said: "I believe in the fact of the atonement, but I do not have a theory of the atonement." That is essentially the position of *The Baptist Faith and Message*, which makes only vague references to Christ's achievement. For example, it says that "in his death on the cross he made provision for the redemption of men from sin." This expression affirms that Christ's death was to save us, but it does not help us to understand how.

There are two reasons why I cannot be satisfied with this

position. One is that it is a retreat from the rich biblical materials. This retreat may be acceptable for consensus theology, but it is not appropriate for any individual who is trying to think about God.

Further, like many other people, I wonder if, in the absence of a theory of atonement, we should continue to affirm the fact of atonement. How can there be any relationship between the past event of Jesus' death and our present experience? To put it bluntly: Why did Jesus die, since all that was needed was for God to say "I forgive you?" In order to answer this question, and because the Bible speaks so often of Christ's death and its meaning, I want to attempt to state a doctrine of the atonement. I am aware that I must make some difficult choices in doing this, and I am willing to bear the responsibility for them.

I have organized what I want to say about the atonement along the lines of the traditional discussion of subjective and objective views. I suggest that subjectively Jesus, by his sacrifice, set an example for men, and he revealed God. He could do these things because he was both human and divine. Objectively he suffered to forgive sins, and he overcame sin. In so doing he dealt with the two dimensions of the human predicament.

Jesus Set an Example for Men

Because Jesus was a real man, God can reasonably expect other men to follow the pattern he set. The pattern was a flawless one. He lived a life of perfect obedience. He always sought the kingdom of God first (Matthew 6:33). He loved God with all his heart, and he loved other men as himself (Matthew 22:34-40). He expressed his obedience when he said: "It is meat and drink for me to do the will of him who sent me" (John 4:34). This is the meaning of Jesus' sinlessness. As we noted in Chapter Five, it is not a negative thing, merely avoiding sins, but a positive one, living all his life as human life is meant to be lived, in obedience to the Father.

The example he set did not stop with his life. It included obedience unto death, even the death of the cross (Philippians 2:5-11). The really remarkable achievement of Jesus was his wrestling with death in Gethsemane, wanting to avoid it like all men, yet praying: "Not my will but thine be done" (Matthew 26:36-45). This was his ultimate example for us: the sacrifice of his life in order to achieve God's purposes. His obedience is a pattern for us.

Jesus said that we should follow his pattern: "If any man would come after me let him deny himself, take up *his* cross, and follow me" (Matthew 16:24-25). And John also spoke of following Jesus' example of sacrificial love (I John 4:9-11). But we may ask: "How can I possibly follow that example?" This question is important. Unless we receive some help we will not be able to follow Jesus' example. This is not a defeatist attitude; it is realistic. Jesus' great example is like the law: it shows us what we ought to be but, taken alone, it does not help us to be that. However deeply we may be moved by his sacrifice, still we do not find ourselves able to obey God as he did. We see his love for people, but we cannot love as he did. We are almost discouraged by his sacrifice, since it seems nobler than we could ever be.

We conclude that by his example Jesus shows us what we ought to be, but we must continue to ask how he helps us to follow that example.

Jesus Revealed God

The Gospel of John opens with a description of Jesus as the Word of God, which means that Jesus was the revelation of God to us. Jesus could reveal God because he was God. A person can be known by others only if he reveals himself to them; they may observe his appearance and other superficialities, but only if he speaks about his plans, his fears, his dreams, can his inner life be known by others. This is even more true of God than of us men. God is known only when he speaks. In Christ he has spoken.

We learn about God through what Jesus said. He spoke of

God's concern for sparrows, of his kingdom (rule over men), of his search for men who are lost (Luke 15). We also learn about God through what Jesus did. By watching Jesus we learn that God loves sinners as much as religious people, that he chooses humble as well as great people, that he welcomes children. We learn that God opposes sickness and casts out demons and forgives sins.

As important as these revelations of God are, still Jesus gave his most profound revelation of God by his death rather than by his life or teaching. By dying he showed us that God is willing to sacrifice himself for the welfare of men. We would never have known this astonishing fact unless Jesus had shown us. His death revealed to us how much God loves us: "Greater love hath no man than this, that a man lay down his life for his friends" (John 15:13). How do we know God loves us? Jesus showed us. How much does God love us? Enough to die on a cross for us.

This revelation of God is a saving revelation to men. Because of our sins we find it hard to believe in God, but Jesus reassures us that God can be trusted. We do not feel loved, and we do not love ourselves, so we are in a vicious cycle of depression and guilt; Jesus breaks the cycle by showing us a gracious, forgiving Father.

But we may ask: "Suppose I do understand God now, does that mean I am saved?" The answer is "no." Better understanding of God, authentic faith in God, is part of being saved, but it is not all of it. Even though we trust God, still our sins need forgiving, and we need to be rescued from our sin. And Jesus' death was for these things too. In fact, unless Jesus does rescue us, there is some question as to whether he really revealed God's love.

What I mean is this. Suppose that a man is sitting on the end of a pier fishing, and a second man runs down the pier shouting: "I want you to know how much I love you." He then jumps into the water and drowns. This is not a convincing revelation of love at all; rather it is the story of a demented and unnecessary act. But suppose that while fishing a man falls into the water and is unable to swim. Then a second man jumps in and pulls him out of the water. In the process of rescuing the drowning man, he himself is drowned. We should regard that act as showing great love, even if nothing was said about love. So it is with Jesus' death. If somehow he was "pulling us out" of our predicament, then his death was also a great revelation of his love. But unless he was rescuing us, it is hard to see how he even revealed his love to us.

Our conclusion is this: these two subjective views of atonement, that Jesus as man set an example for us and that he revealed God to us, need to be supplemented by objective views if they are to be meaningful. We must therefore turn our attention to the ways in which Jesus' death was an objective atonement.

These two ways we will consider are objective in that they do not require a human response. That is, Jesus achieved something by his death which is important for men whether they know it or not. The subjective views of example and revelation picture the atonement as saving us only if we respond to it; the objective views picture it as a finished, saving work for us whether or not we know about it.

The two objective views are objective also with respect to the human problem. As we saw in Chapter Four, the human problem has two dimensions, sins and sin. I believe that Christ has dealt with the human predicament in an objective way.

Jesus Suffered to Forgive Sins

"Forgiveness" is a word with a strong religious and moral ring which nevertheless is frequently used by people who dislike religion. This is because forgiveness plays an important part in the interpersonal relations of most people. Often it is necessary to forgive if a friendship or a marriage is to continue to exist.

Even so, many people who believe in forgiveness feel that the cross of Jesus was superfluous. Their point is a simple one: Forgiveness cannot be purchased, it is free, so why doesn't God just forgive and forget, if he loves us? They agree that men need forgiveness, but they cannot see what the atoning work of Christ could contribute to forgiveness.

Why doesn't God just forgive and forget? Theologians have taken this question seriously. One of them, Leonard Hodgson, has made some positive suggestions about the relationship of the cross to forgiveness. He asks us to consider what possibilities are open to a man who has been wronged. If, for example, a businessman steals his partner's life-earnings, how may the partner react? Hodgson says there are three options. One is for him to forget the whole thing. This is what is often called forgiveness today, but Hodgson does not agree. He says that if he chooses to ignore the crime, two things happen. One is that he becomes implicated in it; the other is that he fails to help the criminal. Hodgson calls this option indulgence, and he argues that a real friend of the offender will not take it.[1]

The second option is to seek to punish the criminal. This option is better than indulgence, for at least in making the moral response of punishment the partner has avoided becoming implicated in the crime. When he reports the theft to the police and testifies against the thief at trial, he cannot in any meaningful sense be held responsible for what happened. Even so, punishment is not a final answer, for it does not take positive steps which may lead to the creative forgiveness of the thief, helping him to become a non-thief.

The third option (which may proceed simultaneously with the second) is to forgive the partner. But forgiveness here is not indulgent "forgetting." It is rather a costly remembering. To forgive in this sense, the offended businessman must accept the painful consequences of his partner's crime. He will feel the pain of betrayal, and he will remain financially poorer than he would have been if there were no crime. Then he will have the right to forgive because he has borne the

[1]See, for example, Leonard Hodgson, *The Doctrine of the Atonement,* chapters 3 and 4.

consequences of the sin. There is no such thing as cheap forgiveness; forgiveness is costly and always involves suffering.

But forgiveness is the best of the three options because it makes possible the restoration of the criminal. If a day comes when the criminal repents of his crime, he does not face the awkward situation of a partner too spineless and too indulgent to be worth being reconciled to, or the wrath of a partner who, though unimplicated himself, desires only to see him suffer for his crime. Rather he faces the prospect of reconciliation with a partner who has manfully accepted the pain of a crime he did not commit and who nevertheless is ready to be reconciled to him and to reinstitute their relationship. In short, the thief faces the prospect of a restoration which will help him to become the sort of person who does not betray a trust or steal from a partner. This prospect, called forgiveness, is available only if the offended partner is willing to pay the price. This forgiveness cannot be provided by the sinner, no matter how repentant he is or how fully he makes restitution of the money he took; it must be provided by the offended partner who pays the price of suffering for sins he did not commit.

I believe that Hodgson is correct. Real forgiveness is not cheap indulgence; it is costly friendship with a sinner. A sinner cannot be helped if others forget his sin or if he tries to do something about it alone. Only if those he hurts accept the pain he causes, can he be helped.

The costliness of forgiveness may be seen even in financial terms in a simple illustration. We have a law in our country against robbing banks. Suppose Joe robs a bank. Our police arrest him, our courts try and sentence him, and he is taken to our prison. How much does it cost us to punish Joe? I expect that we could take away most of his freedom (a great punishment) by building him a $300 cell and feeding him a half-dollar's worth of food daily. Punishment is cheap.

What does it cost to forgive Joe, to help him? A more expensive cell and better food are necessary. We should provide a chaplain to talk to him about his spiritual life and a psychiatrist to talk to him about his emotions. We will provide him a yard for recreation and a library for reading. We will provide a shop in which he can learn a trade so that when he is released he will not be forced to return to stealing. We will provide a television set so that he can keep up with the world outside the prison. We will provide some clothes and money for him when he is released, and we will try to help him locate a suitable job.

But you may object: Why should we pay for all that? He's a thief—he doesn't deserve all that.

Exactly. He deserves only punishment. But he needs forgiveness. He needs the kind of positive, creative help that can be made available only if the community he sinned against is willing to pay the price for him. Punishment is cheap; forgiveness is always costly.

When God is in heaven he is far removed from the sin of man. He does not have to bear the consequences of our crimes in his own life. As I reflect upon the cross of Jesus, I believe that I see God rejecting cheap indulgence and refusing merely to punish wrongdoers. God in Christ was accepting the consequences of our crimes. And how completely did he accept them? To the very bitterest end. When men dealt with Jesus, they did to him all that can be done; they tortured and executed him. And how did he react? By freely accepting it all. Little wonder he could pray while still on the cross, "Father, forgive them, for they know not what they do" (Luke 23:34). And what he achieved for his tormentors he has achieved for all men. He has accepted the pain and thereby provided forgiveness for the sins of all men.

This is not a quantitative transaction; he did not suffer an amount equal to all our sins' consequences. It is qualitative: when he sacrified himself, he had given all that he had. You cannot do more to a man than to kill him. He who has loved us this much has every right to forgive us all freely.

Forgiveness, at great cost, is an objective accomplishment of Jesus by his cross. It has been done for all men everywhere, even for those who, like Abraham and others, never heard about it. It is a fact, an achievement; it is an atonement for mankind. In the words of Jesus: "It is finished" (John 19:30).

But that is not to say that it has become a reality in the experience of every man, for it has not. The father in Jesus' story of the prodigal son always loved, suffered for, and had forgiveness for his son. But the forgiveness was no use to the son until he came to himself and returned to his father (Luke 15). So Christ's atonement is of no value to those who elect not to be forgiven. But we shall talk more about that in Chapter Eleven. Right now we need only to observe that what Jesus did—suffer in order to forgive us—was something objective. Once it was done everything was different for us in relation to our sins.

Jesus Defeated Sin

Our human problem is not just a matter of things we do wrong for which we need forgiveness; it is also a matter of a complex of powers to which we are subjected and from which we need to be liberated.

Much of Jesus' ministry was spent at war with the evil in the world. He healed illnesses, raised the dead, and cast out demons. In an early sermon Peter described Jesus like this: "He went about doing good and healing all who were oppressed by the devil" (Acts 10:38). Jesus occasionally spoke of his war against the forces of darkness.

> If it is by the finger of God that I drive out the devils, then be sure the Kingdom of God has already come upon you.
>
> When a strong man fully armed is on guard over his castle his possessions are safe. But when someone stronger comes upon him and overpowers him, he carries off the arms and armour on which the man had relied and divides the plunder. (Luke 11:20-22)

If Jesus' life was a struggle against the enormous powers of sin, then his death was the climax of that struggle. What was the outcome of the struggle? From earliest times the church has believed that Jesus won a decisive victory over evil. By his resurrection he demonstrated that death was overcome, but even in his dying he was destroying those forces that corrupt our lives and our world. Certainly his victory was proleptic: it was real and decisive, yet it awaited its own climax in the future. But I believe that we can recognize in his struggles and sacrifice the defeat of the enslaving forces.

You may wonder how it is, if Jesus defeated evil, that evil prevails today. And that issue—the apparent success of evil in our world—is certainly the most important barrier to belief in the Gospel. For that matter, it is the most important objection to belief in God. Since ancient times men have found it hard to believe that God cares for them when they see how he allows evil to go on and on. That was the issue raised by the disciples to Jesus when they met a man who was born blind (John 9:1-7). They asked Jesus who was responsible for the man's blindness. Many of us today also ask that question, and sometimes we hear people trying to assign the blame. Jesus responded in two ways. First, he refused to assign the blame. Second, he healed the man. That is the Christian response to evil: We do not try to explain it; we act to destroy it. Explaining evil usually sounds like explaining it away, and Christians must never do that. Evil needs to be destroyed, not discussed. We believe that God has destroyed evil.

Can it really be true that Jesus defeated the forces of evil? Can it be that one day in history God destroyed the sin problem? How can we understand this?

Once I had an experience that helps me to see a little of what Jesus achieved for us. I was playing in a chess tournament in which I was the weakest player. One afternoon my opponent was a mild looking young man whom I did not know. Later on I learned that he held a prestigious place among chess players in universities, but when I played him I judged from his mild manner that he was not a vigorous player.

He checkmated me in eleven moves! After my humiliating defeat he kindly offered to go over the game (we kept records of our moves) to explain where I had gone wrong. I cannot remember his exact words, but the gist of his comments was something like this: "Your first move was good. Your second move was optional but satisfactory. Your third move was weak but not seriously so. But your fourth move was disastrous. You lost the game on your fourth move."

Because I am sometimes a literalist, I responded: "You are mistaken. I did not lose on the fourth move; you defeated me on the eleventh move."

But my opponent was even more literal than I. He responded: "No, Mr. Humphreys, you are mistaken. When you made your fourth move, you were defeated. I won on move four. Nothing could save you then. The game was mine." I accept his word for this, since he knows more about the game than I do.

I believe that the cross was God's fourth move. He really defeated evil that day. He overcame his opponent: he destroyed the enemy. The "game" is his. There is still an eleventh move, a checkmate, out in the future, but the decisive move has been made. That is what Jesus meant when he cried out on his cross, "It is finished." He had won the victory for us. That is why the preaching of the cross is called Gospel, good news—he has defeated the enemy and set us free.

This achievement is a reality, a fact. The forces of darkness will never have the last word—that belongs to God alone, because of the cross. The battle for men's lives is not in question. Christ is true victor, not Satan, and he achieved this by his cross and resurrection.

Both of these objective views of the atonement show us God doing something decisive and final about the human problem. It is of value to men whether or not they know about it.

The older theologians used to speak of Christ's active and passive obedience. He was actively obedient when he voluntarily accepted the Father's will and passively obedient when he endured the tortures of his executors. I am suggesting that in accepting suffering (passive obedience) he was establishing his prerogative to forgive sins, and in defeating evil and death (active obedience) he was liberating men from the forces of darkness.

The weakness of the subjective views of atonement is that they appeal to the good in man—but man is not all good. The strength of the objective views is that they show God dealing with the bad in man. When that was done, then the appeal to goodness also became effective.

We are not forced to choose between the subjective and objective views, for God has both dealt with our sin and sins and appealed to us to follow Christ's example and to know him. We can present a complete Gospel to the world speaking to men in this balanced way.

For further reading:

There is a fine study of the atonement by a Southern Baptist missionary, Robert H. Culpepper, entitled *Interpreting the Atonement*. For a history of the doctrine see Sydney Cave, *The Doctrine of the Work of Christ*. The importance of Christ's defeat of evil was brought to the attention of modern men by Gustaf Aulen in his important study, *Christus Victor*. As I stated above, I found Leonard Hodgson's views on punishment and forgiveness very helpful; see his *The Doctrine of the Atonement*. The most outstanding study of recent years is *The Christian Understanding of Atonement* by F.W. Dillistone.

7. THE HOLY SPIRIT

The achievement of Jesus described in the last chapter was an historical event. It was finished in the first century, and it has a permanent character about it. This permanence is both an asset and a liability. It is an asset because it means that God has really done something about our human predicament. It is therefore a fixed point to which we may turn in faith. It is a finished victory, and this helps us to avoid despair.

But there is also a liability in our claim that God acted in past history. The liability is that as a past event the sacrifice of Christ may become dull, irrelevant, and lifeless. Ancient history tends to be boring because it is hard to see what difference it makes to people today.

How can this liability be overcome? How can the achievement of Jesus in the past be applied to the experience of men in the present? How can an old story become a living, vital message for men today?

The answer to these questions, fortunately, is not up to us. God has answered it. The answer is the Holy Spirit. It is the Spirit's task to take the good news about Jesus and to make it good news for people today.

This is what we see happening on the day of Pentecost too. This becomes clear if we try to imagine the situation of the disciples during those days. For two or three years they had lived constantly with Jesus. Their activities were directed by him. They found fulfillment in being with him and in learning from him. Their fundamental commitment was to be his disciples.

Then, suddenly, he left them. He had tried to prepare them for his leaving, but they did not really expect him to leave, at least not for long (See Acts 1:6). Bereft of his presence and leadership, they were paralyzed into inactivity, unable to begin preaching the Gospel to the world.

All of that was changed at Pentecost. Because Pentecost was a Jewish festival, Jerusalem was filled with Jewish pilgrims from many parts of the Roman empire. On the day of Pentecost the disciples of Jesus who had been inactive and uninvolved in the world suddenly came to life. They proclaimed to the pilgrims in Jerusalem that Jesus of Nazareth, the teacher whom they knew personally, had been executed according to a purpose which God knew beforehand, and that God had resurrected him. He was therefore the true Master of men and the one anointed by God to be the Savior. In his name the disciples offered forgiveness to anyone who would repent of his sins and accept baptism.

What transformed the powerless disciples into aggressive preachers? What gave direction to their lives, helping them to make decisions about what they would do and say? It was the Holy Spirit: "They were all filled with the Holy Spirit." The Holy Spirit brought vitality into the paralyzed group so that they were able to proclaim the Gospel. Then, as the disciples spoke, the Spirit caused the story of the Gospel to become a reality in the life and experience of the Jerusalem pilgrims (see Acts 2).

Pentecost is the event through which the Holy Spirit has been revealed to us. If there had been no Pentecost, we would not have known much about the Spirit. The scattered texts in the Old Testament and the occasional references to the Spirit by Jesus needed the full revelation of the Spirit at Pentecost if they were to be intelligible.

This is important to remember when we try to interpret the biblical passages which deal with the Holy Spirit. Some passages are ambiguous. Sometimes it is difficult to distinguish the Holy Spirit from the human spirit which makes us wonder if the Spirit is divine. In the Old Testament it is often difficult to say whether the Spirit of the Lord is personal or an impersonal force or power. But these difficulties are not decisive if we bear in mind that, as a matter of fact, Pentecost gives us the fundamental revelation of the Spirit.

When we consider Pentecost and ask whether or not the Spirit is divine, the answer is clear. Who came to be with the church at that festival? Not an ideal, not an angel, not the historical Jesus, but God. No other answer seems plausible. Surely it was God who filled the disciples so that they received power. Surely it was the presence of God they experienced. It was not God exactly as they had known him as Jews, nor was it God exactly as they had known him as their leader Jesus. It was the same God, but he was present to them in a new way, in a new experience. Now they understood how God was to guide them in the new era that was beginning. Now they understood that, badly as they missed Jesus, they were not alone. God was still with them.

This is what is meant by saying that the Spirit is divine. Given these considerations it is unreasonable to think that the Spirit could be anything other than God. So the disciples referred to the one present with them as the Holy Spirit, as God's Spirit, and as the Spirit of Christ. Whereas God had been present in their history as Jesus, now he was present in their experience as the Holy Spirit. If the new converts could not know Christ after the flesh, still they knew the same divine presence as the Holy Spirit: "You will receive the gift of the Holy Spirit" (Acts 2:38).

A second major issue is whether we are to understand the Spirit as personal. There are passages in the Bible where it is not clear whether the Spirit is personal, but these should not trouble us. When we recognize that the Spirit is divine, we have an answer to the question whether he is personal. Since God is personal, God's Spirit is personal. He is a person, not a power. The power of the Spirit is more like the power of an influential man who knows how to get things done than the power of an electric generator or of a powerful bomb. He is someone, not something. Paul urged Christians not to grieve the Spirit by their behavior. When we speak of the Spirit we are speaking of the personal God, not of an abstraction, a principle, or a power. Whether we think of the experience of the first disciples at Pentecost or of our own experience today, we realize that the Spirit addresses us, that Christians respond to him as a person, that they live with him in a personal relationship, that they are aided by him in a personal way in their living.

Pentecost teaches us that the Holy Spirit is divine and personal. But what are we to say about him? How can we describe the Spirit of the Lord?

Over the years there has developed a traditional manner of describing the Father, the Son, and the Spirit. It is customary to describe the Father in terms of his attributes (love, holiness, omniscience, omnipotence, and so on). It is customary to describe the Son in terms of the historical events of his life (born of the virgin Mary, suffered under Pontius Pilate, crucified, buried, risen, and so on). And it is customary to describe the Spirit in terms of his activities. In *The Baptist Faith and Message*, for example, he is described as engaged in twelve activities. He inspired the Bible, illuminates readers of the Bible, exalts Christ, convicts, calls, and regenerates sinners, cultivates character, comforts Christians, gives spiritual gifts to Christians, assures Christians, enlightens and empowers the church.

This list of activities is not exhaustive, but it is a good list. We could describe each of these activities in detail, and in fact we will deal with some of them in the next three chapters. But right now I want to make two emphases which I feel are needed today when we think about the activities of the Spirit.

The first emphasis concerns the relationship of the activity of the Spirit to the historical Jesus. I believe that the most fundamental work of the Spirit is to testify to Jesus. When the Spirit came at Pentecost, Peter preached, not about the Spirit or tongues, but about Jesus. The Spirit was present in the preaching of the Gospel. In the Paraclete (Advocate) sayings in the Gospel of John it is clearly stated that the Spirit will bear witness to Jesus (see John 14:15-17, 25-26, 15:26-27, 16:13-15).

Other New Testament writers also speak of the witness of the Spirit to the historical Jesus.

> To prove that you are sons, God has sent into our hearts the Spirit of his Son, crying Abba! Father! (Galatians 4:6-7)

> I must impress upon you that no one who says 'A curse on Jesus!' can be speaking under the influence of the Spirit of God. And no one can say 'Jesus is Lord!' except under the influence of the Holy Spirit. (I Corinthians 12:3)

> This is how we may recognize the Spirit of God: every spirit which acknowledges that Jesus Christ has come in the flesh is from God. (I John 4:2)

In later chapters I will develop some important implications of the fact that the Spirit witnesses to Jesus. Right now my concern is that we see that it is of fundamental importance that the Spirit witnesses to Christ.

If we did not have the story of the historical Jesus, how could we recognize God's Spirit? The concept of the Spirit is like a large container; unless it is filled with the historical content of the story of Jesus, the concept of the Spirit can mean anything.

Where is the Spirit present? Where there is enthusiasm, or successful promotion, or large buildings, or great learning, or gifted personalities, or warm feelings? It is impossible to say. But what we can say is this: The Holy Spirit testifies to Jesus Christ. The Spirit is at work where the Gospel is preached. When the story of Jesus is proclaimed, the Spirit is active. No other test for the Spirit's presence is really trustworthy except this one. I can recognize the Spirit in the lives of those who believe and live by the Gospel.

The other emphasis I want to make about the Spirit's activity is that he brings life and vitality into the experience of the Christian and of the church. He vivifies us. He makes Christian living dynamic as well as decent. The word Spirit is the opposite of the word "dead." The Spirit is wind, breath, a living reality, and he makes us alive. Paul spoke of the *koinonia* (fellowship) of the Spirit (II Corinthians 13:14); the Spirit creates a living society. An early creed rightly described the Spirit as "life-giver."

We will be dealing in the next three chapters with the redemptive activities of the Spirit. For the moment it is enough to notice that all his activities are characterized by liveliness. While liveliness is not a test for the presence of the Spirit (confession of faith in Jesus is the only test), yet it does figure into all the activities of the Spirit. As Paul said: "The Spirit gives life" (II Corinthians 3:6).

For further reading:

A traditional presentation of the Spirit is W. H. Griffith Thomas's *The Holy Spirit of God*, though Leon Morris's *Spirit of the Living God* is more readable. The best theological study by far is George Hendry's *The Holy Spirit in Christian Theology* (Revised). On the question of charismatic experiences the scholarly book by Frederick Dale Bruner, *A Theology of the Holy Spirit*, is excellent, while a popular presentation may be found in Fisher Humphreys and Malcolm Tolbert, *Speaking in Tongues.*

8. SALVATION

Introduction

The word "salvation" has been used in the Bible and elsewhere to refer to several different realities. It may refer to a physical deliverance from bondage, as in the sentence "The Lord saved Israel out of Egypt." It may be used to refer to the sacrifice which Jesus made and because of which he is properly called the Savior.

It also may refer to various aspects in the experience of Christians. Often the Christian experience of salvation is said to have three aspects: past, present, and future. Reformed theology named these, respectively, justification, sanctification, and glorification.

We need to notice that the three aspects of salvation are not alike. The past experience of a Christian, his initial conversion, is a single, fixed event. The present experience is a series of continuing events. The future experience will be a single event. This means that the Christian can say: "I have been regenerated, I am being sanctified, I shall be glorified." Also, the word "saved" can be used for each of these three realities, since all three are part of God's saving activity. Thus we could say: "I have been saved, I am being saved, I shall be saved."

Though this language is odd, still it points to realities. It really is the case that a Christian has been forgiven; it really is the case that day by day God is working to change him into a better person; and it really is the case that one day God will finish the work which he has begun.

We shall talk about the present experience of salvation in the next chapter, entitled, "Christian Living," and we shall talk about the future experience of salvation in Chapter Eleven in connection with heaven. This chapter is about the single, fixed, past event commonly called salvation. It is the initial event in the Christian pilgrimage. When we were children, we used to sing a chorus which said: "Something happened when he saved me." This chapter is about what happened when God saved us.

Although many theologians do not give much attention to the experience called conversion or salvation, I do, and I need to explain why I do. It is because of our heritage. In America and elsewhere, during the Great Awakenings of the 1740's and early 1800's, there were thousands of conversion experiences. Baptists and many other evangelicals are the beneficiaries and recipients of this heritage. Today thousands of people each year experience a crisis in which they trust God to forgive them and to accept them as his children. Since this is our heritage and our experience, we reflect upon it and ask what it says to us about God.

In Chapter Ten we shall be discussing the Baptist view that baptism is for believers. But now we need to observe that churches which administer baptism to infants find themselves in an awkward position vis-a-vis the conversion experience. If, as many of them believe, baptism is an infant's initial step in the Christian pilgrimage and also the time of his regeneration, it is difficult for them to stress the importance of a conversion experience later. Thus in their theologies conversion is not given much attention, however much they may stress it in practice. As a Baptist, I am free to discuss the initial personal response a man makes to God as a salvation experience, for that is what I believe it is. For this freedom I am grateful.

Among Baptists and many other evangelicals the understanding of salvation alternates between two emphases. One emphasis is its freeness; the other is its responsibility. At times evangelicals stress that no one can save himself, no one can earn God's favor, no one can rescue himself or take himself to heaven by his own efforts. Baptists make this emphasis especially strongly against the claims of some Christians that sacraments or especially baptism, or good works, are necessary to salvation. Evangelicals have resisted all implications that a man can contribute to his own salvation.

On the other hand, all Christians recognize that conversion is a moral act of a whole man, and he must be sincere in his acceptance of Christ the Lord. This emphasis is often made today because so many people begin the Christian pilgrimage but fail to follow through on it. Churches today have on the church roll members who cannot be found. Many church members regard their churches as social clubs. In the face of all this a minister is likely to say that becoming a Christian involves a real commitment. Apart from such a commitment one does not have salvation.

So when we describe the initial salvation experience, we face the problem of whether it is free to us or costly to us. We shall try to answer this question in terms of grace and faith.

A discussion of salvation faces another problem too. We are all aware that many factors influence any decision we make: our family, our friends, our society, our past experiences, and our feelings all play their part in our decisions. Making a decision is almost always one step in a series, one moment in a process. Is it accurate, then, to say that there is really *one* moment of conversion?

Certainly the experience of conversion is part of a long process. No one should question this. It is preceeded by a sense of conviction and by the proclamation of the Gospel, and it is followed by a lifetime of Christian living. There is a process.

Nevertheless there is one moment of conversion. If at the time of birth an infant does not trust God, and if at the age of twenty the young man does trust God, then somewhere in between something decisive has happened. Somewhere along the way a line was crossed, a relationship established, a decision made.

The moment itself may have been very obvious. On the other hand, it may have been imperceptible. If a child is very young when he initially trusts God, he may not recognize the importance of his decision and so he may not remember it; it is real nevertheless. If an adult is preoccupied with pressing problems, perhaps family problems or health or financial problems, he may move into the household of faith with little recognition that he has done so. Still, whether his experience is subtle or dramatic is not the issue; the issue is that, as a matter of fact, he has ceased to be a non-believer in Christ and has become a believer.

Other problems present themselves when we try to talk responsibly about salvation. One is that we become so preoccupied with the moment of conversion that we do not give proper attention to the process which led up to it. To avoid this problem we should recognize that before a man ever seeks God, God has been seeking that man. When we did not care about God, God cared about us. As Paul expressed it, "Now that you know God—or rather, you are known of God" (Galatians 4:9).

Another problem is that we may talk about the salvation experience to the exclusion of the Christian living which follows it. It is possible to become so preoccupied with the moment of conversion that we fail to give attention to Christian living, growth, and maturity. We have tried to avoid this by devoting Chapter Nine to Christian living.

We may also misrepresent the conversion experience by too great attention to what was received there. God has done a marvelous thing for us in our conversion. We are very grateful for his gift of love, and our lives are moved by gratitude. But it is not wise for us to talk interminably about what we have received. We must lose our life for the sake of the Gospel. We must grow into the kinds of persons who will be at least as concerned about the welfare of others as we are about the privileges, admittedly very great, which are ours. A proper attention to our benefits is wholesome; undue attention is unhealthy because it is selfish.

So far we have made three points: we are discussing what happened at our conversion though we realize that it is part of a process; we will try to avoid the problems of ignoring the process and of becoming selfishly preoccupied with the blessings of conversion. Now let us see how we may describe this experience.

Our fundamental description will be in terms of grace and faith, for these terms, with their rich biblical and theological heritages, aid us in making a good analysis of the experience. However, before we go to this analysis, we will give attention to the biblical analogies for salvation.

The New Testament contains many analogies for salvation. A comprehensive list would include dozens of items. Here I shall mention four of the major ones as illustrations. The four are justification, reconciliation, regeneration, and redemption.

Each of these metaphors projects a vivid picture. Justification is set in a courtroom; it is the judge's pronouncement "You are found not guilty" that justifies the defendant. Reconciliation is set in the context of human relations; it is the coming together of two estranged people, the resumption of diplomatic relations between two quarreling nations. Regeneration is set in a maternity ward; it is the birth of a child, the beginning of a new life. Redemption is set in a slave market; it is the payment of a price so that a slave is freed from a tyrannical master.

In each analogy the human predicament is seen in a different way, as guilt, estrangement, death, or slavery. In each God's activity is treated in a different way, as a judicial act, a creation of life, the making of a new covenant, or the payment of a ransom. In each the benefits received by a man are different, as a gift of righteousness, a new relationship to God, a new birth, or liberation from sin.

These analogies are typical of many in the New Testament. They are vivid portrayals of the great gift God has given us. To understand them properly we need to notice several things.

One thing is that they all stand for a single reality. They are different descriptions of the single salvation which is ours. It is not correct to treat them as different realities or even as phases of one reality. There is only one reality. There used to be in Reformed theology a doctrine called the *ordo salutis*, the order of salvation, which tried to arrange these (and other) pictures in a specific sequence. Theologians argued about which came first and so on. This is, I think, a mistake. These are various analogies for one reality; there is no proper or improper order. We are free to speak of them in whatever way will call our attention to our need, to God's provision, and to our benefits.

Further, no one of them covers all that may be said about salvation. Some evangelists have tried to treat everything under the heading of the new birth, but this effort cannot succeed. The new birth speaks vividly of our helplessness and of the fresh start of a Christian, but it does not speak at all about the responsibility men bear for their sins or about their response of faith in God.

More recently there has been a tendency to treat reconciliation as the comprehensive description of salvation. This is understandable because the setting of reconciliation (two estranged persons) seems to be the literal relationship of God and man. But no analogy should be taken literally, and no one is comprehensive. In particular, reconciliation does not necessarily speak of the moral dimensions of the human predicament (sins) or of any provision for that dimension. Further, as a one-sided analogy (man needs to be reconciled, God does not) it can degenerate into a vapid, frail description. I have heard it presented thus: "Don't be mad at God; God is not mad at you." When it is put so starkly, we see that it does not speak vigorously of the sacrificial work of Christ or of the importance of the new beginning we experience at conversion. If conversion is merely "not being mad at God" then obviously there is not much to it. There must be a sense of liberation which conversion brings, of the moral force it has in our lives, and of the costly forgiveness without which reconciliation would be simply forgetting our differences.

God And Grace

We are going to analyze the experience of salvation in terms of grace and faith. Paul did this when he wrote that "You have been saved by grace through faith" (Ephesians 2:8).

It is a simple matter to describe what grace and faith are. Grace is the love which motivates God to save sinners. Faith is a sinner's trust in God to save him. We may use a spatial metaphor to see how grace and faith are related to each other: God in grace *gives* salvation, and man in faith *receives* God's gift. Faith is described as "receiving Christ" in John 1:12. More briefly: grace gives, faith receives. It can be put less metaphorically, but more cumbersomely, if we say that God (in grace) forgives men when men (in faith) trust him.

Though these ideas may be stated briefly, it is difficult to grasp their meaning. The difficulty arises because each of these two words has a long history of uses, and many of these uses contradict what we have said above. We are so influenced by this history that we can scarcely free ourselves from it.

For example, grace is often treated as a substance or a power which God distributes to those who need it. This is as true of Protestants as it is of Catholics. "God gives more grace" is often understood almost literally, even by Protestants. Yet if these same people received a letter signed "I send you my love," they would not check the envelope to see if there was an enclosure. We speak of amounts of grace and of distribution of grace in far too literal a manner. We reify grace, treating the word as a reality. Studies are made of *charis* (Greek for "grace") which ignore *agape* (Greek for "love"), and vice-versa, as if we are dealing with the things in themselves rather than with God who loves us and is gracious to us. All this is misguided. When we say that we are saved by grace we mean simply that we are saved by God who loves us. When we refer to "means of grace" or "channels of blessing," we do not mean conduits. We are referring to the fact that God who loves us uses the Bible, or the church, or the ordinances, or a preacher, to help us and to contribute to our spiritual welfare.

It might be good for us, in view of these reifying tendencies, to stop referring to "the grace of God." We might better understand what we are talking about if we refer instead to "the God of grace" or "the gracious God." Many of the really important things about grace become clearer if we speak more directly of God. It is true, as is often said, that grace takes the initiative. We see this more clearly if we recognize that what this means is that God loved us before we cared about him, and he was working to establish a relationship with us before we were interested in him.

It is also true that grace is "unmerited favor." Grace cannot be earned, purchased, or won. But what this really means is that God loves and helps us because that is the kind of God he is; he does not love and help us because we are lovable or because we deserve his help. To say that we are saved by grace not by good works means that we are saved by God who loves us and not by ourselves or by our achievements. It is also true that grace is greater than all our sins. What this means is that God is able to meet all our needs, and he will do this for us because he loves us.

It is important to remember that grace itself does not save; rather God, because he is gracious, saves us. This means that God who loves us acts on our behalf; he saves us by moral action, not by fiat. The world was created by a word, but it was redeemed by an act, costly, decisive, and effective. That act was motivated by God's love or grace.

Man and Faith

Like grace, faith is a simple concept which has become difficult for us because it is covered by many layers of contradictory traditions.

Faith is the response a man makes to God. Since we are now thinking about faith in the context of the initial experience of salvation, we may say that faith is the initial response a man makes to God. He trusts God to save him.

The object of faith is God. Its objective is salvation. Since God was in Christ reconciling the world unto himself, we may say that the object of faith is the Gospel, or even the cross of Christ. What this means is that we trust in God who saved us through Christ, or we trust in God who sacrificed himself on the cross. What we must not do is to believe that any *thing* saves us: the Bible does not save us, nor the cross, nor Christ's blood, nor the Gospel, but only God. We are saved by someone, not by something. We are free to speak of being saved by the cross if we remember that we are speaking imprecisely. To achieve precision we must say that Christ died on the cross to save us.

The objective of faith is salvation. It is possible to trust God for many things—a good cotton crop or dandy weather for a picnic or to heal an ulcer—without becoming a Christian. Our trust must be for forgiveness and life, if it is to be the initial step in the Christian pilgrimage.

Because God loves us (grace) he saves us; we respond to him by trusting him (faith). Clearly the nature of this response is very important. Can it be shown that in the Bible the response to God is faith?

Sometimes today men are asked to make a series of responses in order to become Christians. For example, they are told, first to repent, then to believe, and finally to confess their faith. These are believed to be three steps to salvation. Sometimes they are called a plan of salvation.

The Bible does speak of all three of these, though it never mentions all three together. Further, numerous passages speak of only one, like the famous verse:

> For God so loved the world that He gave his only-begotten Son, that whosoever believeth in him should not perish, but have everlasting life. (John 3:16)

Why is it, then, that other passages speak of repentance (like Acts 2:38) and others of confession (Romans 10:9-10)? I expect that this flexibility is typical of the New Testament. The early Christians did not have a fixed vocabulary to describe their experience with God. Their language was fluid, as it had to be to express what was happening to them.

In a real sense, repentance and confession are the same thing as faith. Repentance to us today often means feeling badly about our wickedness; sometimes we call it remorse or contrition. But in the Bible it often means something different. It means turning to God. It is a metaphor, suggesting a person turning around 180 degrees. And the point is not so much what we turned from as what we turned to: we turned to God. If you translate "turning to God" into less metaphorical language, you may call it "trusting in God." So repentance is the same thing as trust or faith.

This is also true of confession. People utter words and sentences for many different purposes. One common purpose is to express ideas, which is what I am attempting to do now. But we also use words to ask questions, to express our emotions, to stir the emotions of others, to give directions or commands, and for other purposes. One somewhat rare but interesting use of language is to perform acts. There are sentences which *do* things. Philosophers of language call these sentences "performative utterances" because to say the words is to perform the deed. For example, if at an auction you say "I bid five dollars" you have done it: to bid is neither more nor less than this, that you say "I bid." If you have said it, you have done it; and if you have not said it, you have not done it.

I believe that when Paul says that if we confess "Jesus is Lord" he means the same thing as when he said "we believe in our hearts." Confession is not a step after faith (in fact, in Romans 10:9-10 it is mentioned before faith); it *is* faith. To say: "I trust Jesus" is to trust Jesus. Paul was thinking of these words as a performative utterance. Of course, this does not mean that a mute, who cannot audibly confess, cannot trust God. This would be nonsense. It just means that, for many people, to say it is to do it.

So there are no steps to salvation. You may say that we repent (turn to God) to be saved, or that we trust Jesus to be saved, or that we confess "Jesus is Lord" to be saved. Any one is enough, since they mean the same thing.

I elect to describe our initial response to God as faith, since this is a frequently used phrase in the New Testament, and it is useful when we try to relate our response to God's initiative.

What, then, is faith? We have called it "trust" and "belief," but how are we to analyze it? Can we state more precisely the nature of our initial response to God? I believe we can, but I want to be clear on one point. The precision we seek here is not necessary in order to have faith in God. What we are saying now is not to evoke faith but to understand it.

Faith consists of two elements. They are distinct but they ought not to be separate. I would not say that a person is trusting God unless both of these elements were present. As we shall see shortly, it is unfortunate when these two elements are separated. I call the two elements insight and decision. Insight is a matter of knowledge; decision is a matter of will and emotion. Between the two of them, they involve the whole man.

Insight is "getting the point" or "seeing the light." It is catching a vision so that you say: "Oh, I see what you mean!"

The insight aspect of Christian faith means "getting the point" of the Gospel story. What happens is this: when a person hears the story about Jesus, the light dawns on him and he comes to understand what it is all about. His understanding is evoked by the story: "We conclude that faith is awakened by the message, and the message that awakens it comes through the word of Christ" (Romans 10:17). That is one reason why the Gospel is the power of God unto salvation. We must not forget that insight is really a response of the person; no one else's insight will help, each must "get the picture" for himself.

Insight alone, however, is not full Christian faith, because it involves only part of a person, his mind. Christian faith is a response of a total person, his will and emotions as well as his mind. It is possible for a person to say: "I see what you mean about God" without having real faith; he can see the point and still reject it: "I see what you mean—but I won't accept that Savior."

No one can say exactly how much insight is necessary if we are to have real faith. Theoretically it is difficult to determine how much we need to know, but practically there is not a serious problem. The reason is that in a few minutes we can proclaim much more than is required. So what we should do is not to fret about a minimum but present a full, winsome account of the Gospel.

We often meet people who listen but do not get the point. Our procedure there is also clear: we must continue to find ways to express the Gospel over and over until the light dawns for them. Probably very few people see the point at first, and many do not see it for a long time. We must creatively retell the story until they do.

Occasionally we meet someone who sees the point but then asks: "What reason is there for believing that what you say is true?" This kind of response may occur more frequently in the future as more people are affected by the deepening unbelief in our society. There is no easy answer to this question. To answer it at all is to enter into apologetics, which is that part of evangelism which seeks to respond to intellectual difficulties men feel about Christian faith. While we cannot discuss it here, I do want to mention one kind of apologetic response. Sometimes if we will sketch the larger Christian view of the world—God as creator, man as missing his destiny, Christ as overcoming our predicament, the church as God's people, and so on—this may help the person to see why what we are saying is so. It does so in two ways: it touches on many points for which *he* can see the evidence that we see, and also it presents a panoramic view that some people seem to need. While the Gospel is so simple that a child can grasp it, it is also so profound that no one can fully grasp it. Sometimes thoughtful persons need to see it in a larger panoramic form if it is to be convincing to them. We should prepare to make whatever kind of presentation people need.

Sometimes we worry about how critical our understanding of the Gospel should be. I think that, in practice, this is also a simple matter. If a person is critical and thoughtful about other serious matters in his life, then the only kind of insight that will be authentic to him will be thoughtful and critical. If, on the other hand, a person (such as a child) is not critical about other matters in his life, we cannot expect him to be critical in his insight into the Gospel. It is a mistake to ask critical people to become simple or simple people to become critical. A difficulty may develop when a person who accepted Christ uncritically as a child grows into a critical adult; he should be told that his faith (or insight) must grow up with the other aspects of his life and that he is quite free to examine the Gospel in a thoughtful way. No other insight could be of any value to him as a thoughtful adult.

The second dimension of faith is a decision. Having seen the point of the Gospel, we say "Yes" to God in Christ. Decision involves us in a deeply personal way, and the decision to which I refer now is toward God as personal. It is not enough to say: "I believe that story" or "I shall go to church." Rather, we say: "I trust You, God." It is a very personal matter, the beginning of an I-Thou relationship with the Lord. Having received the story about Christ (insight), we now receive Christ himself (decision). Having believed *that* the story about Jesus is true, we now believe *in* Jesus of whom the story speaks.

In order to help people achieve insight into what we are saying, we try to be clear. In order to help them to make a decision about God, we must try to be loving and winsome. Under no circumstances may we coerce anyone into a decision, for that would be our decision, not his and, therefore, useless to him. We must try to help by making the Christian fellowship a desirable one and by adorning the Gospel with good works, but we may not manipulate people in any way.

Full Christian faith should include both insight and personal decision. Occasionally some Christians have favored one without the other, but that does not work out well. Insight without personal decision is merely academic knowledge; it is not the establishment of a genuine personal relationship with God. On the other hand, decision without insight is merely a leap into the dark. There is nothing wise or virtuous about a leap into the dark (though I admit it takes some courage). We live in an age in which people are asked to commit themselves blindly to many causes: try drugs, or buy this stock, or practice transcendental meditation, or put your faith in public schools. We frequently hear: "You'll never know what it is like until you try it." This half-truth is deceptive. No one can fully appreciate something until he has experienced it, but he *can* know enough about it beforehand to make a sensible decision about whether or not he wants to experience it. Few of us can fully appreciate what it is like to be hit by a speeding truck or to take an overdose of drugs or to attempt suicide—but we do know enough to decide not to have these experiences.

God does not ask us to leap into the dark. He asks us to leap into the light. He *reveals* himself in Jesus Christ so that we may gain enough insight to make a sensible decision. When we see the point about God in Christ and then personally say yes to him as our Savior, we are Christians.

We are trying to understand salvation in terms of grace and faith. "Grace" means that God saves us because he loves us; "faith" means that we trust him to save us. Grace is God's initiative, and faith is our response. Often people become confused at this point. They suppose that salvation is somehow an activity in which both God and man play a part: "God provides grace and man provides faith." Or they imagine that faith is something which we give to God in exchange for grace or salvation, as if God said: "I will give you my salvation if you will give me your faith." But faith is not something we give to God. It is not giving at all; it is receiving. Faith says: "I accept God," not "I give myself to God in exchange for salvation." We are not saved by faith at all—there is no such thing as saving faith. We are saved by

God (when we trust him). Faith cannot contribute to salvation, for God provides that at a very great cost to himself; to us it is free. That is part of the meaning of grace: salvation is free.

Similarly, many people describe faith as a commitment. "Commitment" is, I suspect, the most widely-used and the least examined word in the Christian vocabulary today. It has become widely used because many ministers (and others) have become concerned over the failure of many professing Christians to follow through on their initial response. Thousands of people say that they believe in Christ, but they do not practice their Christian faith. To counter this, many ministers have begun to say that faith is a commitment which must be carried out if it is to be real. "It may not take much of a man to be a Christian, but it takes all there is of him." Again: "If Christ is not Lord of all your life, he is not Lord at all." In this sense the Danish philosopher Kierkegaard was right: the last Christian was crucified 1900 years ago. For a commitment is a promise to do something, a pledge to behave in a certain way. If this is true, then salvation is *not* free and faith *is* something we exchange for God's salvation. And if "total commitment" is demanded, then there can be no Christians, for there is a moral ambiguity in the life of every Christian, even the most saintly.

Faith is not a commitment or a pledge to do something for Christ; it is trust in Christ who has already given himself for us. As we come to appreciate his love more and more, we shall respond with more and more gratitude, not to live up to a pledge, not to avoid falling from grace, not to be sure our faith was big enough, but simply because we appreciate what God has done for us. Commitment is very important to Christian living, but it is not something we do in order to receive salvation. For that we trust God.

Those who believe that somehow faith is a swap or a commitment which saves us have tried to insist that salvation is all God's work anyway. They do this by saying that faith is itself a gift to us from God. This is very misleading. Of course

God created us, so all of our life is a gift from him. Also, the Gospel story helps us to gain the insight and then make the decision to trust God. Even so, faith is really *our* response; it is not literally a gift from God. If it were, then presumably there would be no response for men to make to God. But God calls on us to make a response. We trust God, and in saying this we do not jeopardize in the least the fact that salvation is entirely God's work, for we recognize that our faith does not save us, only God does. We may put it in this way: "I trust God to be my Savior." That is all there is to it.

We can summarize this chapter as follows: God loves us (grace) so he sent Christ to sacrifice himself to save us (Gospel); we hear this story and see that it is true (insight) and so we decide (decision) to trust God (faith): we trust him, and he then accepts us as righteous (justification), restoring our broken relationship with him (reconciliation), creating a new life in us (regeneration), and liberating us from the powers to which we were enslaved (redemption). Salvation is God's work in the life of a person who trusts him.

For further reading:

An excellent study of grace is Samuel J. Mikolaski's *The Grace of God.* Some of the metaphors for salvation are treated in Leon Morris's *The Apostolic Preaching of the Cross,* though in another context than the one in this chapter. For a different understanding of salvation than the one I have presented, see Dietrich Bonhoeffer's *The Cost of Discipleship.* The definitive study of forgiveness is *The Christian Experience of Forgiveness* by H.R. Mackintosh.

9. CHRISTIAN LIVING

Introduction

I have deliberately avoided calling this chapter by the customary phrase "The Christian life" because I believe that this phrase is misleading. I do not think there is any such thing as "the Christian life" in the sense of *one* proper way for a Christian to live. I think there are many ways which a Christian may properly live. When God created men, he did not make them all alike, and there is no reason to believe that when he saves men he makes them all alike.

But, you may ask, if there is not one proper way to live as a Christian, then what will be the common factor which makes different ways of living to be Christian. The answer to this is found in the Gospel.

A Christian is a person who has heard the good news story that God was in Christ, reconciling. He has trusted this God to be his own Savior, and so he has become a member of God's family. What all members of the family have in common is the Gospel and their experience of trusting Christ.

Many different kinds of people have this faith in common, and they live in different ways. In our study of Christian living we are not going to begin by expounding how they ought to live; we are going to begin by asking how, as a matter of fact, Christians do live. We shall examine with care some of the ways that serious Christians live today. Our examination will not be comprehensive; there are millions of

Christians and it would be impossible to analyze all the nuances and refinements which these millions of believers practice.

What I will do is to distinguish some of the major orientations to Christian living. I believe that I can discern five different orientations to Christian living. They are not completely separated from one another, of course, and many readers will recognize aspects of their own Christian living in several of these ways. Even so, these five ways are distinguishable from one another, and there are Christians whose lives completely fit into one or the other of these ways. We shall consider the five ways one by one.

We must begin with several points firmly in our minds. These five ways are all Christian and all good. We are not discussing bad Christian living in this book; enough is said about that elsewhere. We are discussing good Christian living, the living of serious, thoughtful believers in Christ.

Further, we are not going to suggest that any one of these five ways is superior to the others. I do not think any one is. All five are good, and no one way is more mature or more spiritual than the others. It is true that an individual Christian may move from one of these ways to another, but he should not assume that this proves one way superior to the others. All that he has proven is that for *him* one way is better than another. For some people one way is superior to another. I would go further and say that for some Christians one way would really be intolerable while another way is very helpful. But we must not universalize our experience and try to make all other Christians become like ourselves.

All five of the ways have strengths, and we shall try to stress these. All five also have large issues which are capable of becoming serious problems. These issues should be faced squarely. In facing them we may seem to be critical of the serious dedicated living of God's people. But facing the potential problems is important. It will help us to overcome them. Just because I do respect all five orientations, I want to face the problems so that those who live in these ways may avoid them. We shall avoid misunderstanding if we approach these ways with the attitude that they are not exclusive, that no one way is superior for all Christians, and that each one contains real strengths and real or potential problems.

The First Way

The first way of Christian living is oriented toward rules and institutions.

Christians who live this way believe that God has given us certain rules or principles which we follow in order to live as Christians. It is not that they feel that Christians happen to follow these rules; it is rather that they believe that Christian living is neither more nor less than this, but it is precisely this: keeping the laws of God.

Also they feel that God has established certain institutions, and Christian living consists of being loyal to these institutions. God has established the church, so a good Christian is one who is a loyal church member.

Many Christians who live this way might accept the following description of a Christian. A Christian is a person who has made a public profession of his faith in Christ. He is a church member and, where possible, a church leader. He supports his church by attendance, money, and loyalty. At work he is honest, and at home he is kind. He believes the Bible, reads it occasionally, and studies it if he needs to do so for personal reasons or to fulfill teaching duties. He blesses his food and may occasionally say prayers privately. He will not be caught in worldly activities like adultery or drunkenness.

Not all Christians who follow the first way are alike. Some of them may emphasize discipline and the development of strong character. They may say: "God wants us all to do our duty." Others may stress successful church work. They may say: "God wants us to evangelize our community, and we must organize and work to reach all the people with the Gospel and to bring them into God's house." Others may stress humble service to people. They may devote themselves unselfishly to serving as Sunday School teachers, or they may form an informal committee to welcome newcomers to the community. Still others will stress enthusiasm: they feel that the success of church work is God's business, but their own role is energetically to share the joys of being a Christian. All these emphases have in common the idea that God tells us what to do, and Christian living is doing what he commands.

There are two outstanding strengths to this way of Christian living. One is that it takes very seriously the moral demands of the transcendent God. God does give commands, and in an age when people are not inclined to accept any demands it is refreshing to meet these Christians who are so earnest about God's demands.

The second strength of this way of Christian living is its nobility. People who live this way are really committed. They are not lukewarm disciples, but they are living in total seriousness. They are to be appreciated for their serious discipleship.

This way of Christian living also faces several problems. One is that many Christians find it difficult to motivate themselves to live in this way. They may have a weak sense of duty; they may be repelled by the idea that fear, or even duty, is a suitable motive for Christian living. For whatever reason, they do not feel compelled to spend their lives keeping rules and supporting institutions.

Perhaps it could be put this way. If something could happen so that the rules and institutions were transformed so that Christians could feel positively about them rather than negatively, then they could try to live this way. If the rules were not so oppressive, if they did not tend to legalism, if they were beloved like the law of God in Psalm 119, then many more Christians might be able to live this way. We shall discuss later on how this transformation can occur.

A second problem concerns the results of living this way. Unfortunately the results are always open to failure. If a Christian succeeds in keeping the rules, then he stands in jeopardy of becoming self-righteous; if he fails to keep the rules, he is likely to become so discouraged that he quits trying to live like a Christian at all. Success and failure both have dangerous tendencies, and many Christians face both the dangers. Many Christians swing like a pendulum from despair to arrogance, with a measure of hypocricy thrown in to counterbalance the despair. Rules tend to do that to human beings, and Christian rules tend to do it to Christians. Like the first problem, this one can usually be solved only by the transformation of the rules so that Christians feel differently about them.

Another problem faced by this way of Christian living concerns the sense of aloneness. Many Christians feel that it is just at the point of keeping God's laws that they most need help. But this way does not really provide help. The only help it knows is to say that God gave the rules so we must keep them. This sense of aloneness and helplessness becomes apparent in the prayers of Christians who live like this. They often pray because they feel they ought to do so—that is a revealing fact in itself. A child who talks to his family only because it is his duty to do so clearly does not experience a close family relationship. For many Christians prayers may be warm and spontaneous in giving thanks or in worship. But when they come to make requests for God's help in their lives, either they hesitate or stumble, or else they become very formal. The reason for this is that in this way of Christian living no provision is made for God to help us in our weakness. Christians often feel alone in their pilgrimage, and they do not know how God can help them.

The other four ways of Christian living are reactions to this first way. Each of them stresses that God is present and active in the life of the Christian. God does more than tell us how to live; he helps us to live as we should. Religion is more than morality; Christian living includes keeping rules, but those rules must not supplant God.

The first way correctly recognizes that a Christian's life is a gift from God; it correctly recognizes that a Christian's life should be lived for God; but it often fails to see that a

Christian lives his life with God. It is this failure that the other four ways try to correct. They differ primarily in how they understand God's presence and activity.

The Second Way

The second way of Christian living is oriented to miracles. God wants to do miracles in our living. If we live in a way that is open to his doing miracles, then our living is Christian.

This way of Christian living is the simplest of the five to describe. The first thing to observe is that for the second way Christian living does not just happen to include miracles, it *is* living for and with miracles. The best known preacher of this way is Oral Roberts. He is not just saying that God does miracles; he is also saying that living for miracles *is* Christian living.

The chief ingredient in the second way of Christian living is faith. But it is faith of a certain kind, not just faith in general. Obviously it is a faith in miracles, but it is more. To believe that God can do miracles is not enough; to believe that God has done miracles in the past is not enough; to believe that God may do a miracle in my life now is not enough; I must believe that God is going to do a miracle in my life today. That is the faith that we need as we live day by day as Christians. Oral Roberts calls it seed-faith; he means that we plant this faith as a seed, and God will cause it to grow up and bear a miracle in our lives.

This way of Christian living has several strengths. Its obvious strength is its openness to God's sovereign power. People who live this way really believe that the Lord is in control of the world and that he is able to intervene on behalf of his children. This faith is not the only kind of faith, but it is to be respected in a world that is quickly becoming secular, pagan, and gullible about idols.

The second way also has several problems to face. One arises from its peculiar understanding of faith as "expecting a miracle." Expectation is always in danger of becoming presumption. "Seeding for a miracle" may degenerate into demanding a miracle. That is something faith must never do. In the Bible the emphasis is never on demanding things of God but on requesting them. In our zeal to encourage people to have faith in God's miracle-working power we may sometimes imply that they have the right to expect a miracle. No one has this right. Authentic faith may ask for a miracle, but it does not demand one. In the New Testament a demand for miracles is consistently rejected (Luke 11:16; 23:8-9; Matthew 16:1-4). Jesus refused the devil when tempted to cast himself down from the temple expecting God to send angels to rescue him.

A second problem for this way of Christian living concerns the priority given to miracles. The Bible records many miracles of God, but it does not place excessive emphasis on them. Jesus warned that a wicked generation sought after signs, and Paul spoke with disapproval of Greeks who seek wisdom and the Jews who seek a sign.

Miracles have great subjective importance. If you are in a desperate financial condition, miraculously receiving money seems very important to you. But objectively, in the eternal purpose of God, miracles seem to play only a small part. We must not overestimate their value. Sometimes we may feel that our faith would be greatly helped by a miracle, but quite possibly it would not. Or we may feel that we could easily evangelize our community if God would only do one great miracle. This simply is not true (see Luke 16:31). Miracles do occur, but we grow accustomed to them and they change things very little if at all. More people are drawn to Christ in one small Baptist church in one ordinary week than were attracted by all the great attention given to an apparently miraculous appearance on a screen door in Texas a few years ago. Extraordinary miracles get some attention; but the ordinary proclamation of the Gospel is what helps men to trust God.

So those who live for miracles must learn to recognize their true place in God's activity. They must add to their seed-faith other kinds of faith for Christian living.

Another problem about this way of Christian living is that it pushes God into gaps in our lives. Because the extraordinary is stressed, not much attention is given to the ordinary. Naturally when a Christian escapes from a serious car wreck without injury, we say that God has protected him. But what do we say when a Christian is injured? Naturally when twenty people join our church on a Sunday, we believe that God is at work in our midst. But what do we believe when twenty leave our church on a Wednesday evening? Naturally we trust God when we pray for a Christian with cancer and she is healed and lives for a long time. But what happens to our faith when a Christian dies?

My conviction is that God is with us in all of life's experiences. We mislead people if we select a special group like miracles and say: "There God is at work."

Finally, as a matter of fact, we ourselves do not cease to function in between miracles. Oral Roberts and others who preach this way of Christian living know what to do when a miracle is not happening. I think that Christians need to hear not only about how to live when miracles are in progress but also about the back-up system we live by when there are no miracles. In other words, let us have some realistic talk about Christian living during the times when God is not doing a miracle.

If the second way of Christian living could confront these four problems—by avoiding presumption, minimizing miracles, seeing God as always active, and spelling out the back-up system we use when God doesn't do miracles—it could provide great help to the many people who try to live as Christians in this way.

The Third Way

The third way of Christian living is oriented to God's control of the Christian's life.

Many Christians who begin their living in the first way become discouraged. Some of them believe that the secret of Christian living lies in the discovery that we cannot live as

Christians on our own. The key to Christian living is then described as letting God take control of our lives. Only if he takes over do we have any hope of success as Christians. The battle is too hard for us, the race too swift, the journey too long; we must let God do everything through us.

The secret of Christian living, then, is to be submissive to God. We must throw off our sinful (and futile) independence and become completely dependent upon the Lord. We must be emptied of self so that Christ can occupy the throne of our lives. We must be broken and humbled in order to be filled with God's power.

This way of Christian living has many assets. One is that it recognizes God's presence in all of life, not just in rules or miracles as the first and the second way do. God is present in all of life, and this way helps by insisting upon that. It is especially useful because it teaches us to face life's problems in the strength of God.

A second asset is its recognition of the Christian's dependence upon God. It is true that we cannot do any good apart from God. We do need him every hour.

But this way of Christian living also faces some problems. The first concerns the attitude which a Christian is supposed to cultivate toward himself. Does God really want us to cultivate dependence, to deny such abilities as we have, and to be broken and emptied? I doubt it. I believe that many passages in the Bible encourage us to struggle valiantly with life and its problems, to behave courageously, and to use our skills to serve God. We are not taught that our powers are either sovereign or worthless; we are taught to take a sober measure of them. We are not taught to deny our own feelings and thoughts. To deny oneself means to avoid selfishness; it does not mean to act as though I were a thing rather than a person.

Another related problem is how we are to act towards the problems we confront in our lives. This way of Christian living transmutes all problems into one: the problem of dependence upon God. Dependence on God is commended as the solution to all problems. But all problems are not just that one, and dependence upon God is not a magic cure for all our problems.

If at the end of a month you have $500 in the bank and $600 in bills you are not necessarily a sinner; you are broke. God may want you to face up to your financial problem—as a financial problem—responsibly and in a Christian way. If people do not talk to you and wander away when you come up, you are not necessarily a backslider; you may be a bore. God may want you to behave maturely in facing up to the matter of relating well to others. If you feel like you are odd man out, different, and everyone is out to get you, you are not necessarily unspiritual; you may have a touch of paranoia. God may want you to face your feelings about yourself and others and to learn to accept yourself and to trust the good will of others.

My point in all this is that while we should see God as present in every area of life, we should not assume that that means that all of life's problems are really spiritual ones in disguise. Some are not. And we should not expect that affirming our dependence on God is the only response we must make to our problems. We may be asked by God to act, to speak, to think, to study, to struggle, to discipline ourselves, and many other things, as well as to be broken and humbled.

Finally, this way of Christian living must face the problem of what it considers to be the most ideal relationship between God and a man. This third way not only affirms that God's control of our lives is the way to cope with life; it seems to affirm that God's control of our lives is the ideal of Christian living. I doubt this. I know that God is sovereign, but I believe that in his sovereign grace he intends to do something more important with us than to control us. I recognize that God may occasionally use a man as an instrument of his will, but I do not think that is the final purpose of God.

Men were created and redeemed, not just to be used by God, but to be in fellowship with God. God wants us finally to be, not in his possession, but in his communion. His ultimate concern is to relate to us as persons, not as things.

Those who teach the third way of Christian living need to take into account the ultimate purposes of God. They need to teach people that, beyond brokenness, there is Christian fulfillment. They need to remind their followers that God asks us to lose ourselves because he intends for us thereby to find ourselves. Otherwise, the teaching about being controlled by God is a half-truth and misleads Christian people.

The Fourth Way

The fourth way of Christian living is oriented to the will of God. It rests upon a conviction that God has an individualized plan for the life of every Christian. Christian living consists of finding and doing God's will. This is sometimes called being in the center of his perfect will.

People who live this way do not agree about how detailed God's plan for their lives is. Some of them insist that God plans even the smallest details of our lives, like what tie we should wear or whether we should include salad in tonight's menu. They support this conviction by reminding us that what seem to be small matters may have large consequences. Nevertheless, for our purposes here we shall be considering God's will in larger issues like marriage, vocation, whether and where to go to college, where to live, and the like.

If Christian living consists of finding and doing God's will, then the devoted Christian will want to seek God's will earnestly. Several techniques have been developed for finding God's will. Since the Bible does not tell us specifically what God's will is ("Joe, marry Sue"), seeking God's will may mean reading the Bible in a special way. A young person trying to decide whether or not to go away from home to attend college may pray: "Lord, as I read your Word, show me what to do." When he reads in the Bible the words "Thou shalt surely go," he interprets this as God's will for his life.

A second method for discovering God's will is through prayer and meditation. While praying, a Christian may have a strong feeling that God is calling him to become a minister.

This sense of "being led" would ordinarily be described as a hunch or an intuition, but in the context of this fourth way of Christian living it receives great prominence as God's way of directing his child. Not only intuition but other forms of leadership are described in a special language. It is a language replete with words and phrases that have a meaning that is easily understood only by those who have had the experience of "being led." To the outsider it almost seems like a mystic experience.

A third method by which God's will is sought is by praying for God to open or close doors. A young lady who is uncertain as to which of two marriage proposals to accept may ask God so to arrange things that the wrong offer is withdrawn and the offer "in God's will" remains. When God shuts all the doors but one, the young lady believes she has discovered God's will.

A closely-related method for finding God's will is called putting out the fleece. (It receives its name from an Old Testament story found in Judges 6:23-40.) It consists of asking God for a sign which will confirm his will. A young man who is thinking about joining the Army may pray: "Lord, if I pass my physical let that be a sign that I should join." Sometimes the sign requested may be more like a miracle. A missionary with no prospects of receiving money may ask: "Lord, if you want us to add a wing to our infirmary, send us $5,000 this week."

A final way for discovering God's will is known as waiting upon the Lord. It is said that often we make decisions too hastily, running ahead of God. We must learn to be patient if we want to discover God's will. Discernment may come if we delay our decision.

Once a Christian has discovered God's will, he will be able to do it. Armed with the secret of knowing God's plan, it is a straightforward matter to follow it through.

This way of Christian living has many advantages. One is that it is keenly aware of God's presence in the decisions of life. We are not alone as we make the choices that will determine the course of our lives.

A second strength is its dedication to doing God's will. Christians who live this fourth way do not ask to know God's will so they may decide whether or not they want to do it; they consider that wicked. It is assumed that they will do God's will once they discover it. This commitment is very commendable.

This fourth way of Christian living also has some problems. One is that it may encourage Christians to evade decision-making. In its fine effort to affirm God's presence in the decisions of life, it may, in effect if not in intention, lead Christians to refuse to make decisions. One man told me: "I have only one decision to make, and that is the decision to let God make all my decisions." I believe this is a mistake, because I think that sometimes God wants us to make our decisions, to really make up our own minds for ourselves. In Chapter Four we said that God created man with freedom; freedom is something God wants us to have. Christians who refuse to make their decisions are rejecting God's gift of freedom and therefore thwarting God's will—not doing it. The techniques for discovering God's will may camouflage our refusal to accept his will when we make our decisions. "Waiting on the Lord" may be simple procrastination; "putting out the fleece" may be an evasion of responsibility. What God wants is not mindless, indecisive children, but persons who, trusting in the Lord, will stand on their own two feet, make decisions, and accept the responsibility for their decisions. Christian living does not make us less fully persons but more fully persons. Those who teach that Christian living is doing God's will should expand their description of Christian living to include the idea that God calls on us to make choices.

Freedom is often praised today, but it is such a terrifying thing that few people seem really to want it. I believe that God wants to give us more freedom than most of us will accept. He thrusts freedom and responsibility on us, but often we run away from it. We should at least be repentant about our refusal to bear responsibility and not try to say that God wants to make all our decisions for us. There are times when God has a plan for our lives, but the Bible does not teach that God plans everything for us. Even when he does plan things, he may not choose to inform us of his plans; we must go on living responsibly and making the best decisions we can.

A second problem which this way of Christian living faces is the leveling of all decisions. If God has a detailed plan for us, then any detail of our lives is as important as any great matter. If God plans our menus, we should make an ultimate commitment to eating what he wills. But the details of life are not that important. Part of our growth as Christians is that we learn what really matters in life. Persons are more important than things or programs; what shirt we buy is not as important as whether we love our family and are loyal to our friends.

When Christians tell me how impressed they are with God's concern over the details of life, I can agree. But when they seem to feel that the details matter as much as the great issues of love, trust, and truth, then I cannot agree. We need to be more discriminating than that. I have known Christians who allowed what they believed to be God's choice of a spouse for them to guide their conduct more than what the Bible teaches us is God's will regarding our marriage relationship. On the evidence of the Bible I just don't know if God has a plan about whom each of us should marry, but I do know that it is God's will that we love, trust, and treat with kindness the one whom we do marry. I do not know if God has selected for every Christian a special job in a certain city, but I do know that he wants Christians to work hard, to be honest, and not to follow destructive vocations. I do not know if he has chosen a certain college for each young person to attend, but I am confident he wants college students to live seriously, to study, and to try to share the Gospel with others.

So this way of Christian living needs to set some priorities and not become so infatuated with God's detailed plans that it misses his great purpose, shown in Christ, of creating a society of good persons. It must not lose sight of the forest in its preoccupation with the trees.

The Fifth Way

The fifth way of Christian living is motivated by gratitude; its major emphasis is on loving persons; it trusts God to be present and active in our lives in a particular sense; and it involves our living life fully.

This way of Christian living rests on the conviction that God has freely forgiven us and accepted us in his Son Jesus Christ. We feel sure that God is our Father; we are not afraid of God. Our assurance about God is possible because as we think of the Gospel events we know that God loves us. We recognize that it is by his love that we exist, that we are redeemed, and that all good things come to us. So we feel profoundly thankful for his goodness. Out of our gratitude we want to live like good Christians.

We believe that of all the things God has created on earth, the greatest is persons. All other human activities are secondary to our loving other people as ourselves. We want to understand, accept, and if possible help the persons we meet day by day. Whatever else God's will may be, we know that he wants us to become lovers. We believe that love is the fulfillment of all requirements of the law.

To love is to have at heart the interests of another. Love is not necessarily a feeling; it is a behavior. It is acting toward another person with concern for his welfare. It is not sentimental or lustful; it is thoughtful and concerned. Jesus commands it; Paul praises it; the cross shows us what it can ultimately achieve. For this is love, not that we loved God, but that he loved us and sent his son (See I John 4:7-11).

This way of Christian living includes a certain kind of trust. It is trust that God is with us, that we are not alone. It is trust that our life is not only from God and for God but with God. It is also trust that God is active in our lives. He is not merely a spectator; he is doing something. What he is doing is redemptive.

In the previous chapter we said that salvation is both past (finished), present (ongoing), and future (yet to come). The essential trust valued in the fifth way of Christian living is trust that God is at work redemptively, changing us. Every day is a day of salvation; every day God works in us to transform us more into Christ's image; every day we are fashioned more into good persons.

This faith is different from faith that God is going to do a miracle or faith that God has a plan. It is trusting God to work in a saving way in our lives. I believe that God does this.

God's redemptive work is not only in us. He also works through us to change others around us. That is what it means to be a channel of blessing. Also, he works in a redemptive way with the events of our lives. When bad things happen, he can take them like raw material and transform them into something good. He can change evil into good; that is what redemption is. That is the meaning of the verse that says that all things work together for good to those who love him (Romans 8:28). It is not that things which seem to be bad are really good. They are really bad, but God changes them into good.

As we are trusting God to be active redemptively in us, we live our lives completely. This means that we affirm life; we do not negate it. We throw ourselves into the earthly matters of life; we do not set ourselves off in religious corners. Like Christ, who was born in a manger not a church, and who ministered in the public places not in the temple, we are immersed in the life of our time. While we may have to be critical at times of this life, still we are involved in it.

Living life completely includes at least four activities. One is that we think for ourselves. We do not believe that it is spiritual to be ignorant. We do not feel that faith is the absence of knowledge. We believe that God wants us to use our minds, to think for ourselves, and to be informed. He has created a huge inanimate world of rocks and oceans and space, all mindless; he has given us minds and he wants us to use them. There is a place for authority in this way of Christian living, but there is no place for an authoritarianism that is mind-destroying. The Bible often praises Wisdom; Jesus taught us to love God with all our minds, and Paul often prayed for understanding and knowledge. That is why we believe that we must think seriously and carefully for ourselves.

Second, living life completely means feeling our feelings. It means being aware of our emotions and accepting them for what they are. It does not mean pretending they do not matter, and it does not mean camouflaging them with unrealistic words, spiritual or otherwise. If we have emotional problems, we should try to cope with them. We may need to learn to love ourselves; many Christians never do. We may have to control our anger while trying to search out its sources and to discover ways to express it without harming ourselves or others. We may have to deal with all the fears and insecurities that come from recognition of our own finitude: we feel insecure because we may die, we may lose our health, or we may be unable to feed our families. We must learn to accept these and other fears. Our feelings, like all the rest of our lives, come from God. Living life completely means living with our feelings.

Third, living life completely means making our own decisions. We said earlier that some persons who claim to live by God's will may be avoiding decision-making. Now we say that many times what God wants is for us to make our decisions. In all the world only human beings can decide things in freedom; God made us this way, and he wants us to be this way. In making decisions we do not worry about missing God's will. If God has a plan for us, and if we are trusting him and living life completely, we will not miss his will. He will see to that; he can be trusted for that. If he has a special job or college or spouse for us, he will work that out if we will live life fully, trusting him to be with us.

Growing up means learning to accept the responsibility for decisions we make. Unless we do this, we remain stunted in our development. God wants us to learn to make decisions, to make them wisely, and to live with their consequences.

What if we make a poor decision? The adult answer is that we make the best of it. Everyone makes wrong decisions sometimes, even the Christians who say that God has shown them his will. There is no way to avoid mistakes, so we must learn to accept them too.

Fourth, living life completely also means coping with our problems. We do not try to transform them into spiritual problems with spiritual solutions if they are really not that. If they are financial, we deal with them in a responsible financial way. If they are emotional, we deal with them as emotional. If they are social, we cope with them as social problems.

Sometimes our problems are spiritual. We may need to repent of selfishness, or to return to a Christian fellowship, or to study to learn more about God, or to seek guidance if we are confused. But if our problems are with our parents, we try to learn to relate better to our parents. If we are in poor health, we go to a doctor.

As we live life completely—thinking our own thoughts, feeling our feelings, deciding on our decisions, and coping with our problems—we are trusting God to be acting in a redemptive way. He is in all life with us and through it all, and he is changing us into good persons.

This fifth way of Christian living faces one important problem. It concerns God's activity. If we are to live life so completely, then how can we believe that God is really active? What is the relationship between our living (which seems to be a hundred percent) and God's saving work (which seems to be a hundred percent)?

This is a paradox. As we saw in Chapter Five, D. M. Baillie called it the paradox of grace. As Christians we believe that every good thing comes to us from God; we also believe that food we worked for and cooked is a gift from God. The fact that we are fully involved does not mean that God is any less involved.

For many of us this is difficult. Sometimes we try to divide things up: I pray/ God does miracles; God plans/ I follow. Or we may see God and ourselves as sort of cooperating on projects, as if he provides the brains and we provide the muscle. But the truth is that these are not true images. God is active in the midst of our activity. As we live life fully, God redeems us. We do not believe that the less we do the more God does; we believe that the more we do the more God does.

We can best see this, perhaps, by reading Galatians 2:20 as a series of balancing statements, followed by a summary.

God's Work	My Work
1. I have been crucified with Christ.	Nevertheless I live.
2. Yet not I, but Christ lives in me.	And the life I now live.

Summary

I live by trusting the
Son of God who loved me
and gave himself for me.

Christian living is a paradox. We are to function independently (live life fully), yet we are always completely dependent on God (to redeem us as we live). We cannot divide up life into divine and human parts. We must accept the paradox: "I live by trusting." God is at work in Christians who are living life fully.

A Theology of Christian Living

Theology is thinking about God. If we are to have a theology of Christian living we must ask the question: What understanding of God is held by Christians as they live their lives?

For the first way of Christian living, the way oriented to rules and institutions, God is understood as a Lawgiver. He tells the Christians what to do; Christian living is doing what we are told.

For the second way of Christian living, the way oriented to

miracles, God is understood as a Miracle Worker. Christian living is exercising seed-faith in God; God then does miracles.

For the third way of Christian living, the way oriented to God's control of our lives, God is understood primarily as Controller. He takes control of the life of the Christian; Christian living is accepting his control by being dependent.

For the fourth way of Christian living, the way oriented to God's will, God is understood primarily as a Planner. In theology this is called Providence. God plans our lives; Christian living is the discovery and following of his plans.

For the fifth way of Christian living, the way oriented to God's redemptive work, God is understood primarily as Savior. He is at work changing the Christian into a better person; the Christian lives his life completely, trusting God to be at work in all of it.

All five of these understandings of God are true. God really is Lawgiver, Miracle-Worker, Controller, Planner, and Savior. But God's saving work takes precedence over his other activities. He may or may not give rules, do miracles, take control, or plan our lives: that is optional. But if there is to be any hope for us, it lies in the fact that God is saving us. All the other four works are auxiliaries to salvation. They all contribute to his saving of us, to changing us into good persons. That is the purpose and justification of his other activities.

I think that, if we see this, we can understand why it is not absolutely essential for us to live in any one of the five ways. Whichever way we live, God will be doing his saving work in us. Perhaps he wants us to give attention to some other phase of his work at some time.

What we do need, though, is to acknowledge the priority of his saving work. We need to see that rules are not capricious: they are to help us be better persons. Miracles which God does are not merely displays of power: they are to help us be better Christians. God's control of our lives is not the negation of ourselves as persons: it is to help us at a particular place where we need it, to become more like Christ.

God's plans are not secrets God wants us to decipher: they are his providential care for us on our pilgrimage toward Christian maturity.

Similarly, we are not to expect him to give a rule for every occasion; he may or he may not. We cannot expect him to do a miracle whenever we feel we need one; he may or he may not. We cannot expect him to take control so we can fall into childlike dependence and still live like Christians; he may take control or he may not. We cannot expect him to plan every detail of our lives; he may or he may not. What we can expect is that, as we live our lives, he will be at work redeeming us. We trust him to be redeeming us.

In traditional theology this is called the doctrine of sanctification. I believe that it is true. God has saved us once for all in Christ; now he is at work in us transforming us into better Christians.

For further reading:

While many books treat Christian living devotionally and inspirationally, few deal with it as a subject for theological reflection. Good examples of the first way of Christian living are Luther Joe Thompson's *Monday Morning Religion* and David Mason's *The Compulsive Christian*. For the second orientation see Oral Roberts, *The Miracle Book*. For the third, Jack Taylor is good; see *The Key to Triumphant Living*. Of several examples of the fourth, perhaps Paul Little's booklet *Affirming the Will of God* is best. The fifth way is presented in books like Keith Miller's *Taste of New Wine*.

10. THE CHURCH

The Reality of the Church

Men who believe in God realize that the church is a reality. They do not say: There ought to be the church, or Let us pray that there will be the church, or Let us work so that there may be the church. Rather they say: The church is a reality.

The reality of the church is derivative. The church is real because God is real. Without God there could be a religious society but there could not be the church. Therefore, the church is a reality of the second order. God is the first-order reality.

Since the reality of the church depends upon the reality of God, we think that the best way to understand the nature of the church is to ask how the church stands in relation to God. By viewing the church in relation to God, we sense the overwhelming reality of the church, and we come to see what the church really is.

But what is the church in relation to God? This is a hard question, not because it is difficult to find a description of the church, but because there are so many descriptions to choose from that it is hard to know where to begin.

Often these various descriptions are mixed together in a way that leads us to *feel* strongly about the church but does not help us to understand the church clearly. This is true of some of the hymns we sing. For example:

> The church's one foundation is Jesus Christ her Lord;
> She is His new creation, By Spirit and the Word:
> From heaven He came and sought her to be His holy bride,
> With His own blood He bought her, and for her life He died.

In this one stanza the church is described as a building whose foundation is Jesus, as a new creation, as the bride of Christ, as a purchase which Jesus made, and as a corpse come alive. Sorting out these various images, and other ones in the New Testament, helps us to understand more fully what the church is.

Biblical scholar Paul Minear of Yale Divinity School has studied the New Testament pictures of the church with great care. In a book entitled *Images of the Church in the New Testament* he distinguishes ninety-six New Testament analogies for the church, four of which he regards as of special importance. With so much material to work with, where shall we begin?

We choose to begin by asking the question, "What is the distinctively Christian understanding of God?" The answer is this: The distinctively Christian understanding of God is that God is Father, Son, and Holy Spirit. Let us try to understand what the church is like by seeing the church in relation to the Father, the Son, and the Holy Spirit.

The Old Testament tells the story of God choosing a people for himself. The relationship between Jehovah and the nation of Israel was summarized this way: "I will be your God and you will be my people." Thus the activity of God was that of election, and this was primary. Because God chose Israel, Israel became God's people. This is beautifully described in the seventh chapter of the book of Deuteronomy.

> For you are a people holy to the Lord your God; the Lord your God chose you out of all nations on earth to be his special possession.
> It was not because you were more numerous than any other

> nation that the Lord cared for you and chose you, for you were the smallest of all nations; it was because the Lord loved you and stood by his oath to your forefathers, that he brought you out with his strong hand and redeemed you from the land of slavery, from the power of Pharoah, king of Egypt. (Deuteronomy 7:6-8)

The same relationship which existed between Jehovah and the nation of Israel in the Old Testament is said in the New Testament to exist between God and the church. God chooses the church and the church is God's people. Thus Peter could write of the church: "You are a chosen race . . . You are now the people of God who once were not His people" (I Peter 2:9-10). We begin to understand the church when we realize that God has chosen the church to be his people. That is what we say first: The church is God's chosen people. And when in faith we seek to understand what this means, we begin to realize that it really is so. God chose us long before we ever chose him. God was looking for us when we were not looking for him. When we found God, in reality it was because God has found us. And so, having been found by him, we are his people. Theologian Claude Welch describes this relationship as the *convocatio* and *congregatio* of the church: the convocation or call of God and the congregation or coming together of a people. The church is a new race of men—a people characterized by the fact that God has selected them. That is the first thing we say about the church: The church is God's chosen people.

What is the relationship between the nation Israel, God's people in the Old Testament, and the church, God's people in the New Testament? It has to do with the nature of God's initiative and work. His work may be described as shaped like an hour glass: First, he intended to use all mankind, and when they failed, he planned to use the Jewish people; when they failed, he planned to use a faithful remnant, and when they failed, he used his servant Jesus. Jesus succeeded. And since Jesus succeeded, God could use those who were followers of Jesus, the church.

This brings us to the second aspect of the church, the relationship of the church to Jesus, the only-begotten Son of the Father. The relationship is this, that Jesus sacrificed himself to create the church and the church has thereby become the body of Christ upon earth. Just as the Father first chose the church and then the church became the Father's people, so the Son first gave himself on the cross and then the church became his body upon earth.

In a recent book by C. H. Dodd, Jesus was described as the Founder of Christianity. That is true, but as important as that fact is, the church is more intimately related to Jesus than other religions are to their founders, for by his sacrifice Jesus does not simply found the church, he constitutes it. He does not simply initiate the church, he gives it reality. The church is a reality because of the Gospel events.

To the church Christ has given the task of carrying this Gospel with all of its liberating power and its implications for the life of mankind, to every man. Through the church Christ continues the work he began while he was here upon earth. While on earth Jesus worked through his body as every man does; today the ascended Jesus works upon earth through the church which is his body. The church is now the body of Christ upon earth. Paul said to the Christians at Corinth: "You are Christ's body, each of you a limb or organ of it" (I Corinthians 12:27-28).

God chose the church, and so the church is God's people. Christ died for the church, and so the church is the body of Christ, serving Christ in the world. Furthermore, the Spirit regenerates the church, and so the church is the fellowship of the Spirit. The Father chose the church in eternity. The Son died for the church in history. And the Spirit regenerates the church in experience. God's work is not all in eternity and not all in the past; it is also a present spiritual reality. The Holy Spirit gives life to the church today, and so the church is the fellowship of the Holy Spirit.

In the third chapter of the gospel of John, Jesus spoke of a man's being born of the Spirit. In an early creed the Holy

Spirit is described as the Lord and life-giver. It is this regenerative, life-giving activity of the Spirit, illustrated by the unusual events on the day of Pentecost, which makes the church a living reality.

Man without God is dead through his moral sin; the Spirit comes and gives to dead men new life. The Holy Spirit fights against the deadening affects of formalism, moralism, and legalism. He brings to the church a share in the life of God.

Because the Spirit has given the church life in this way, the church is a fellowship which is made possible because the Spirit has given them a common life.

We may summarize what we have said about the reality of the church in this way:

the Father chooses, and the church is his people,
the Son atones, and the church is his body,
the Spirit gives life, and the church is his fellowship.

The first word to be said about the church always concerns the activity of God, not the activity of man. We must realize first of all that God elects in eternity, that Christ dies in history, and that the Spirit regenerates in experience. This is the organic aspect of the church, the divine activity which constitutes the relationship of God to the church. The church is the elected, the atoned-for, and the regenerated.

The second word to be said about the church concerns man's response to God's activity; the church is the people of God, the body of Christ, and the fellowship of the Spirit. This is the covenantal aspect of the church, its relationship to God in view of its response to God's activities of election, atonement, and regeneration. The church's response to the initiative of the Triune God is to be a people, a body, and a fellowship.

What does it mean to say that the church is a people? It means that these men are not isolated individuals who just happen to be together, like a group who happen to be on a bus together. They belong together, they are one race, one nation, bonded together by God who chose them. Christian people *are* one people. It is their responsibility to behave like one people. They are to think of themselves as one people, not as isolated individuals or groups.

What does it mean to say that the church is Christ's body? It means that through this people Christ is doing his continuing work in the world. This body has work to do. The church is to serve Christ faithfully and effectively. It is not here without a purpose, nor is it free to choose its own purposes. As Christ's body it is to do the work he chooses for it. Because the church is the body of Christ, individuals in it are to work together in harmony like the limbs and organs of a human body. A Christian is not to be proud of his superior gifts but to realize that his gifts are to be used for the doing of Christ's work. No Christian is to be ashamed of his gifts, but he is to use his gifts to serve Christ. No Christian can demand that all other Christians be like himself, for Christ did not mean for all to be alike. What all are to have in common is not the various individual gifts, but the supreme gift of all: *agape* love.

This brings us to another question: What does it mean to say that the church is a fellowship? It means that this is a community of love. These people are friends. They accept one another, for through the Spirit they have a life together.

There is one final question about the reality of the church. Is the church all this in reality, or is this wishful thinking? Do these elaborate images really fit the church? The answer is that the church really is like this, but this can only be seen with the eyes of faith. How are we to understand these gifts of God, when what we seem to see around us is so different? And how are we to reconcile the fact that the church *is* Christ's body with the fact that the church must *labor* to serve Christ as his body? Can we put these together, even when we have faith in God?

The solution to this becomes clearer when we think about the situation of an individual Christian man. What do we say of a Christian: Is he a sinner or is he righteous? He is a sinner: he does wrong, he is not perfect, he is still rebellious.

And yet he is righteous: for Christ's sake his sins are forgiven, he has been justified by Christ's sacrifice, he is God's own child. Martin Luther was right when he described the Christian man as *simul justus et peccator*, at the same time both a good man and a sinner.

The same paradox holds true of the church. The church is a people, yet it does not behave like God's people, and it must be told to behave like his people. The church is Christ's body through which he works, yet the church does not always serve Christ as his body, and it must be told to serve like his body. The church is a fellowship, yet it does not act like a fellowship, and it must be told to live together in mutual love and acceptance.

There is a great paradox here, and it may be seen only by men who have faith that *God's work is the ultimate reality of the church*. A sociologist may investigate the people called Christians, but only a Christian can know that this people is God's people and that it is God's people precisely because God chose them to be his people. A politician may see that the church is a large body of men, but only a Christian can know that this body is Christ's body for whom Christ died and through whom Christ works. An outsider may see that the church is a fellowship but only a Christian realizes that this is a fellowship of the Holy Spirit because the Spirit breathed life into the church.

Because a man without faith cannot see the reality of the church like a Christian can, he does not realize that there is a paradox about the church. There is a real sense in which the church is invisible to him. The world can know that the church is present, but it cannot know the spiritual reality or nature of what is present.

The Presence of the Church in the World

Up until now we have discussed the church without reference to time or place. If you asked of the church as we have described it, "Where is it?" or, "When is the church like that?" we would have answered, "The church is everywhere and it is always like that." And it is. But the church does not remain everywhere in general at all times generally; it also appears in a particular place at a particular time. It expresses itself in one particular place at one particular time, for example, as the First Baptist Church of a town in Mississippi in 1974. By this concrete expression the church comes into focus. It is no longer a blurred abstraction. The local expression of the church impresses upon us all what we need so much to realize: the church is a reality. Because it is here and it is now, we give it our attention, and we become aware of the presence of the people of God.

It is important to notice that a local congregation is not just a part of the great Church like a slice out of a pie. Rather, a local congregation is an expression of the entire church. The First Baptist Church is not only a part of the church, but it is the expression of the one true church. When St. Paul addressed his letter to Corinth he spoke of "the congregation of God's people at Corinth." There was a congregation of God's people at Corinth so that the church would have a tangible presence in the pagan city.

When you see a congregation of God's people in a local time and place, you see the church expressing itself. We have described the church as a people chosen by God, the body through which Christ works constituted by the sacrifice he made, and the fellowship called into being by the life which the Spirit gives. This elect people, this Gospel body, this regenerate fellowship expresses itself as a local congregation. A local congregation is a people chosen of God, redeemed by Christ's sacrifice; it is his body through which he works, and it is a fellowship made alive by the present Holy Spirit.

Every Christian ought to be a part of a local congregation which is an expression of the church. It is essential for a Christian to be in the church, and it is also essential for him to be in a local congregation which is an expression of the church. Christian faith is profoundly personal, but it is not private; it is a social matter. To be God's child is to be a brother of all other children of God. The Bible knows nothing of solitary religion. Christians who attempt to isolate themselves from the church are hurting themselves. Christ works with us through his body the church, and if we do not accept his work through the church, then our spiritual condition will suffer. A man may prefer to spend Sunday morning fishing rather than at church, and he may claim that he can meet God on the lake. Now no one can say that God is not on the lake, for he is. But the point is that if a man cuts himself off from the body through which Christ works, he cuts himself off from the ministry which Christ wants to perform for him through the church.

Some Christians would agree that we all need to be part of the church, but they question whether a local congregation is the best expression of the church. They may even wonder if it is a very good expression at all. Perhaps they believe that other Christian groups are superior to the local congregation. Maybe they are young people in the Youth for Christ movement, or men in a Gideon's group, or students at a seminary, and in these groups they feel that their needs are met and they have all the fellowship they want. Why should they bother to be a part of a local congregation? First we should realize that each of these is a fine group, each has a ministry to perform for the Lord, and we appreciate them all. But my judgment is that, excellent as these groups are, they cannot take the place of a local congregation. The reason for this is that they do not express the church as well as a local congregation does. A local congregation is open to all kinds of believers, and so it shows forth the universality of the church, whereas these organizations are for particular groups. They are exclusive rather than inclusive. Youth for Christ is for young people not older ones, the Gideons is for men not women, and seminaries are for ministers not laymen. But the local church is for every kind of Christian: young or old, man or woman, clergy or laity, rich or poor, black or white, wise or simple.

This is the genius of the Christian church: It is open to all men, not just to one special group. The Lord wants it this way because he loves all men and because all men need to be in fellowship with all kinds of other men. The old need the enthusiasm of the young, and the young need the experience of the old. The rich need the patience of the poor, and the poor need the rich to pay the bills. The wise need the down-to-earth attitudes of the simple, and the simple need the teaching of the wise. Most of the human relations on which people become involved are with compatible groups, and often this means no more than that "birds of a feather flock together." But it is God's desire to overcome all the artificial separations between men, not by whittling everyone down until all are alike but by making each man like Christ so that he will accept all men, even those unlike himself.

Somewhere in the world there needs to be a fellowship of men based only on this love which Christ has brought to us, and the church is that place. In the church all kinds of people come together because they belong together, they need each other. Everyone suffers when segregation of any kind becomes a way of life for Christians, because all Christians stand in need of each other. All Christians need to bear testimony to the fact that God has broken down the barriers that separated men from other men. Groups like Youth for Christ, Gideons, and seminaries render important services to the church, but only a local congregation can demonstrate the universality of God's love and meet the needs of men to live together with other men dissimilar from themselves.

If we accept the importance of a local congregation, then we must ask what a local congregation is like. The Swiss theologian Emil Brunner, in his book *The Misunderstanding of the Church,* made a distinction between the church which is an institution and the *ekklesia* which is a fellowship. Although Brunner's exact position is somewhat obscure, he seems to be saying that fellowship is the really important matter and the institution is secondary. A fellowship uses an institution. His point is that a misunderstanding of the church has occurred because people have supposed that the church is basically an institution.

Put in this way, Brunner's point makes sense. Certainly the life of the church is the important thing and the structure of the church is secondary. But we ought to notice that without structure, life cannot be effective. In order for a fellowship to achieve anything it must institutionalize.

Suppose, for example, that a Christian young person goes off to a college where he knows no one at all. On arriving he learns that his roommate is also a Christian. The roommate introduces him to two other Christian friends. They can sit around in the dormitory room talking about the joy and privilege of being God's children. They have fellowship without any sort of institution. But suppose they want to do something together. Someone suggests that they form a Bible study. Then questions begin to come up: Where shall we meet? When shall we meet? How often shall we meet? What part of the Bible shall we study? Who will lead the study? In order to have a Bible study they must set up a structure or institution. It is very simple structure but nevertheless it is a structure. It is not set up to squelch their fellowship; in fact it is set up to assist it. Let us say that they decide to meet in Bill's room Tuesday night at 9:00 o'clock to study the book of First Peter. They will take turns leading the study, and Bill will lead it on the first night. We can see clearly that there is nothing wrong with this simple institution, though there is a danger that some people will take a wrong attitude toward it. For example, some of the students could become so concerned about how many people attend the study each Tuesday night that they cease to care about making the study a good one.

The problem in the church today is not so much in its institutions, though no doubt they could be improved. The real problem is that some people have wrong attitudes toward the institution, they love the institution for itself rather than seeing that it is the means by which the fellowship does its work. Unfortunately, there *are* local congregations whose primary concern seems to be to keep the institution going. We ought to beware lest we become slaves to an institution. But the proper response to this problem is not to destroy or desert the institution; it is to use it for its true purposes. It is as mistaken to think too little of the institution as it is to think too highly of it. If we remember that institutions are inevitable for action, then we will not pretend that we can do without them. Rather we will structure them so that they are efficient, and we will use them for the work we believe in. It is as mistaken to desert an institution as it is to become its slave. People who hope to create a fellowship by destroying an institution are bound to fail, for the fellowship they seek to create almost inevitably will substitute a new institution for the old one. What is needed is a new attitude, a realization that the fellowship is God's gift and that his people can work through the institution.

A local congregation, then, is basically a people, Christ's body, a fellowship, which constructs and makes use of certain institutional forms in order to do its work. Now the question is, which form? What should be the structure of the church as it expresses itself in history?

There are three basic forms of church government. The Roman Catholic, Greek Orthodox, and Episcopalian churches all have an episcopal form of church government. Episcopal church government is an oligarchy. A relatively small group of men, the bishops, assumes the responsibility for leading the church. They are a self-perpetuating group because they alone can consecrate other men to the bishopric. In the past, episcopal church governments have claimed biblical authority for their system, and they especially treasure the episcopal succession which traces an unbroken chain of ordinations from the New Testament apostles until today.

The second form of church government is presbyterian. Presbyterian church government is representative government, very much like the government of the United States. An elected body of men, usually called elders, assumes the responsibility for leading the church. Presbyterian governments often claim biblical authority for *their* system.

The third form of church government is congregational. It is practiced by Baptists and others. Under this form the responsibility for all church matters rests upon the entire congregation, not upon a small group either elected or self-appointed. Congregationalists have found support for *their* system in the New Testament. Which of these structures is the correct one?

From the studies of biblical scholars it now has become clear that there were several forms of church government in the New Testament, not just one form. Eduard Schweizer wrote: "There is no such thing as *the* New Testament Church order." [1] Thus, a careful student can find support for each of the three forms of church government in the New Testament, and he can find also aspects of each form of church government which do not appear in the New Testament. The episcopal system is supported by the appearance of a ruling function among the New Testament *episcopoi* or overseers, but it cannot demonstrate that the episcopal succession goes back to the apostles or even that a succession of ordinations would have been a matter of importance to anyone in the New Testament era. Presbyterians can demonstrate that older men or elders (*presbuteroi*) held a position of authority in some New Testament churches, but they cannot identify these men with elected leaders like the seven men referred to in the sixth chapter of Acts. Congregationalists may point to the fact that St. Paul appealed to entire congregations at Galatia and Corinth rather than to ruling officers when he called for doctrinal and practical decisions to be made. But it is not possible to demonstrate that every local congregation in the New Testament era had one pastor and several deacons.

This variety of forms of church government in the New Testament produces some confusion, but the case is not hopeless. In theory some conflicts remain unreconciled, but in practice we are on surer ground. If it is our intention to follow New Testament pattern, then we ought to be willing to accept a variety of forms of church government just as men in the New Testament era did. We should show no more anxiety over this variety than did the early Christians.

[1]Eduard Schweizer, *Church Order in the New Testament*, p. 13.

Also, we should take a pragmatic attitude toward many aspects of church life. We do not need a biblical precedent in order to have a business manager in a local congregation. If a business manager can help the congregation to minister more effectively, they may have a business manager. In all this we should be open to God's leadership whether through straightforward congregational decisions, gifted individuals, or the press of circumstances. For it is certain that God, who is always free to do as he chooses, has used these various church structures in the past, and it is likely that he will continue to do so in the future, perhaps using others as well.

We have said that local congregations are the best expression of the church. Now we ask: What ought to be the relationship between local congregations? We have said that we should follow the example of the New Testament and be willing to live with a variety of forms of church government. If that is so, then what should be the relationship between local congregations which are not like each other? How should the Baptist, Methodist, and Presbyterian congregations of a Mississippi town be related to each other? It is true that they share one life, but how do they express this unity?

Concern for Christian unity sometimes has been restricted to affirming the notion of an invisible spiritual unity. By itself this is not satisfactory, any more than the idea that the love of Christ in Christians should be an invisible spiritual virtue. Love must act and express itself, as John pointed out in his first epistle. Similarly it is necessary for the unity of Christians to express itself. There are other men to whom the concern for Christian unity has meant institutional ties between churches and denominations at the highest organizational levels. By itself *this* is not satisfactory, for the emphasis is too much on the unity of the institutions and too little on the unity of the people of God. Perhaps authentic Christian unity might be carried forward more successfully and realistically if attention were given to the relations between local congregations.

The situation is this: In order for the church to be focused in history, it has expressed itself as local congregations. These congregations are a good tangible presence of the church, but because there are so many of them, they seem to imply that God's people are divided, when the truth is that God's people are one people. Further, these congregations are not all alike in structure, but each one is an expression of Christ's church, and so they share a unity which overcomes this dissimilarity. How can they express this unity tangibly? They should express it by treating each other as friends rather than as opponents or competitors; by being humble about whatever gifts they believe they have and generously sharing these gifts with one another; by realizing that though the church should be protected against heresy and sin, it is both heretical and sinful to refuse to fellowship with one's brothers; by continually remembering that every Gospel church is God's work and is to be respected as such; and by sharing in the tasks to which all are summoned by God. This is possible when local congregations take seriously the prayer of Jesus as recorded in the seventeenth chapter of the Gospel of John:

> But is not for these alone I pray, but for those who through their words put their faith in me; may they all be one: as thou, Father, art in me, and I in thee, so also may they be in us, that the world may believe that thou didst send me. The glory which thou gavest me I have given to them, that they may be one, as we are one; I in them and thou in me, may they be perfectly one. Then the world will learn that thou didst send me, that thou didst love them as thou didst me. (John 17:20-23)

The Mission of the Church

The mission of the church is part of the church's privilege. God has honored his church by calling her to share in his great work in the world. A society, like an individual, can suffer from a sense of uselessness when there is no important task it feels called upon to perform. God has blessed the church by commissioning her to do his work in the world. The church is the body through which Christ acts today.

The church does not obey God out of fear but out of faith. She serves, not to earn God's acceptance, but because she is thankful that God already has accepted her. The Methodist theologian R. Newton Flew was correct when he wrote: "The Church is in the first place the object of the divine activity, and then the organ or instrument of God's saving purpose for mankind."[1] The church is those men in whose hearts God's Gospel has done its saving work, and thus the church is also those men through whose lives God's Gospel can go into the world to continue its saving work.

Some Christians do not regard the mission of the church as important. On the one hand, some evangelicals have tended to stress the individual and his responsibilities instead of the church and its mission. Surely each Christian is called to discipleship. But discipleship is not a solitary life; it takes place with other disciples. On the other hand, more liberal Christians have had a clear vision of the social aspects of Christianity, but they have lost sight of the distinction between the church and the world. Of course, God works wherever he pleases, but he has chosen to work through the church. In other words, God first saves men and then he works through those men to save others.

What is the mission of the church? Any statement of the church's mission will be arbitrary, but even so a statement is needed. We shall describe it as the worship of God, evangelism and service to the world, and the edification of itself.

In Psalm 29 we read: "Give unto the Lord the glory due unto his name; worship the Lord in the beauty of holiness." Among the items which together make up the mission of the church, we put worship first, because we believe that it is proper always to see the vertical relationship before all others.

The church cannot worship God alone and unaided. "Let the people praise Thee" is a prayer for God to help his people to worship. We can only worship God as God helps us, so it is no credit to us when we worship. Jesus spoke of a time coming soon when "those who are real worshipers will worship

[1]R. Newton Flew, *Jesus and His Church*, p. 24.

God in spirit and in truth" (John 4:23). That is the church, the real worshipers. When the disciples asked him how to pray, he opened his prayer with worship: "Hallowed be thy name" (Matthew 6:9).

To fail in worship is to fail in a critical area. Worship is indispensable to the church. If we do not *as a people* direct prayers full of praise, honor, reverence, adoration, loyalty, and thanksgiving to God, there is something missing from the life of the church. There is no substitute for worship, for corporate worship; evangelism is not a substitute, nor is enthusiasm, or great learning, or even private worship: "Let all the people praise Thee."

Worship is an end in itself, and it requires no further justification than that God is God. We do not go to church simply to receive benefits from the Lord; we also go to give to him the honor due his name.

True worship must not be regarded as a means to an end. We know that we cannot earn God's approval by worship, but do we see the sinister danger that lurks in the slogan: "The family that prays together, stays together—Worship together this Sunday"? I favor families praying and staying together. I also believe that corporate worship can have a cohesive effect on a family. I even accept that there are many people whom it is legitimate to call to worship by presenting the benefits worship may give them. But I am convinced that in the end there is only one legitimate reason to worship God, and that is because God is worthy of our praise. If we do not think he is worthy, that is, if we do not have faith to believe him thus, then we shall be playing the hypocrite to worship him. And sooner or later we shall get the uncomfortable feeling that what we are saying amounts to shameless flattery and that God must be terribly self-centered. What the church needs is faith in God, so she can worship him in her innermost heart and with integrity, or, as Jesus said, in spirit and in truth. It is the need for this kind of faith that led Martin Luther to say, "Faith is the true worship."

The church of God worships because the goodness and love

of God demand her worship. She does not worship merely because she feels like it. She does not wait to feel, she is moved by her faith to worship God. When God is God in the church, the church is at worship. The God whom the church worships is the Holy Father of Christ, and Christ the Savior, and the Holy Spirit.

We do not have to become Jewish to worship, any more than we have to become Roman Catholic. Christian worship is evangelical. By this I mean that the God whom the church adores is the God who was in Christ, reconciling the world unto himself. The praise given to God is for God's great redemptive act in Jesus Christ. The thanks given to God is unto him who gave his life for us. Christians do not lay aside their experience of salvation in order to worship God, for the God Christians worship is he who is their Savior and who desires to rescue the world from the arms of the evil one.

There are various kinds of worship, various ways to worship. If we sing "Holy, Holy, Holy" to God and not only to ourselves, that is worship. Worship may be expressed in other less formal music, of course; the experience of worship varies, the reality endures. Worship may be high or low; that is dispositional and is not important. The learned musician and theologian Albert Schweitzer danced to the music of jungle drums in Africa. There is no "holy" music; the church may use whatever music helps her to worship God in spirit and in truth.

We should not reduce worship to other activities: "I worship by my life." Let us join with Isaiah and see the close relation between the worship of the seraphims and the commissioning of Isaiah to be a prophet. Service and worship are closely related, but they are not identical. If the church comes together in genuine adoration of God, she may then go out to serve God well.

Experimentation in worship is good, even if some of it proves to be a failure. But it must help us—not to feel good—but to worship God. Can we worship in our churches? Is there a time and place for the people of God to honor the

Lord? Let us hope so. Let us plan to make it so. For worship is not optional to God's people. "For it was his will that we, who were the first to set our hope on Christ, should cause his glory to be praised" (Ephesians 1:12).

The second aspect of the church's mission is evangelism. It is not, on the surface, self-evident that men should propagate religion (all religions do not do so). Part of the genius of the Christian faith is that those things which are most precious and important to us, namely the events of Christ and his death and resurrection, are capable of being shared with all men, of being proclaimed for what in truth they are, Gospel. And so to evangelize is endemic to the Christian faith. If we care for the world, and if we really believe the Gospel, then we shall evangelize.

We may define evangelism as making faith a possibility to men today. All that we can do in that direction, we must do. This includes the way we live. But if we really want to make faith a possibility for men today, we cannot restrict our evangelism to living; we must speak. For there is no doubt but that the Gospel helps men to believe, and that telling about Christ generates a situation in which men come to trust God. Before I became a Christian I heard that God loved me, but I was not interested. Then I heard that God loved me so much that Christ died for me, and I became a Christian. Before I was a Christian no one presented the Gospel to me. When someone told me, I trusted Christ. Love is expressed by acts. The Gospel was an act, and evangelism is an act. Both are acts of love which help men to respond to God. Human moral response is made to the moral *act* of God in Christ and to the moral *act* of someone speaking to us, not to an abstraction called love.

In order to be evangelistic the church must walk a thin line between two errors. On the one hand there is the danger of manipulating people; on the other hand there is the danger of ceasing to take the initiative in speaking to men about Christ. Manipulation occurs whenever we treat people as impersonal objects and force them to do our bidding. Many Christians associate the word "soul-winning" with manipulative techniques for getting people to respond to the Gospel. If "soul-winning" refers to a loveless, depersonalized activity, the term should be dropped, though I am not sure that it is always used in this way.

True evangelistic preaching is not a form of propaganda. A propagandist does not care about truth or about his audience as persons. He cares only about success, and success is measured by the number of others who do his bidding. A serious Christian evangelist, on the other hand, is convinced of the truthfulness of his message. And he is not seeking just any sort of response from his hearers. He does not want and will not accept a programmed, mechanical response from men. He seeks a personal, moral response. He asks men *as men* to turn from sin to God in Christ. He sees men as persons, not as fodder for church work. He avoids and discourages manipulation.

Some Christians, in an effort to avoid manipulation, have gone so far as to give up taking the initiative in presenting the Gospel to the world. This reaction is too extreme. The church today must not forget that in the book of Acts the newborn Christian church was characterized by a loving aggressiveness. The church did not hide itself from the world in fear or in pride. She did not wait for the world to come to her for advice or love. Rather she went out to the world with a message of God's love and achievement in Christ. The church today must keep that initiative, being careful not to become manipulative in the process. How can this be done? No rules can be laid down; evangelism is an art not a science. But generally it can be said that if evangelism is marked by love and concern for the men who do not know Christ, it will find a way to take the initiative without being manipulative.

There are many ways to evangelize. The church must explore new forms if she is to be effective. New forms are required by a changing world and by the fact that there are many different kinds of Christians. Each Christian must find his own metier, his own pace. Some Christians are extroverts;

others prefer a less dramatic way of living and of evangelizing. Let each one find his pace and his way and share the Gospel. There is a place for evangelism of the hard-sell variety; it includes direct language, a manly presentation, an earnest plea. There is also a place for soft-sell evangelism which is more leisurely, subtle, and relaxed.

There is another thing too: In the Scripture (Ephesians 4:11-19) some men were said to be evangelists especially, while others were called pastors and teachers. Every pastor ought to be a teacher and evangelist. Evangelists should do their part in teaching the people they win to Christ because evangelism is a first step, not a last step. Even so, each Christian has his special work, and Christians should respect those whose calling is not identical to their own. In short, each Christian should do his own work and respect the work of others, knowing that Christ is at work through his entire body, of which the Christian is one member.

Too often evangelism has been understood as a one man job. Individuals do it, of course, but they are supported by the church. More important, the fellowship of the church is the most effective tool for evangelistic work. Men today are busy but bored, talkative but lonely, and the Christian fellowship draws them like a magnet. A fellowship is evangelistic.

When the church has shared the Gospel with the world, she has not done everything she can to help the world. In the world some men are sick, some uneducated, some enslaved, some lonely. The third task of the church is to meet the needs of men other than the need for the Gospel.

The church, like the Christian, must find its life by losing it. The church must serve the world. She will grow more if she *stops* planning her own expansion and starts planning to meet the needs of men. She will be stronger if she gives herself unselfishly to men who need her help.

In this, as in all the aspects of her ministry, the church follows Christ's example. Christ preached, the church preaches. Christ taught, the church teaches. Christ healed, the church heals. In church buildings, schools, and hospitals, the church is following the Lord's leadership. When the church tries to survive by promoting herself, she defeats herself. But if she serves hungry, friendless, discouraged men, she will be victorious.

In the church some men have favored service at the expense of evangelism. But no Christian who believes the Gospel can really love an unbeliever and not tell him about Christ. On the other hand, no Christian who shares the Gospel can really love a man and not care about the physical, emotional, and social needs of that man. Faith works by love. There is no real dilemma here: When people are lost, the church should proclaim the Gospel, when they are hungry, she should share her food, when they are lonely, she should be their friend. It is as wrong to have evangelism without service as it is to have service without evangelism.

Service is not merely an arm of evangelism, any more than worship is. The church does not feed hungry men simply to get them to accept the Gospel any more than she holds a worship service simply to get Christians to preach the Gospel. The church worships because God is worthy of her worship, and she feeds men because they are hungry, and she preaches the Gospel because it liberates lost men. No one ministry excludes or dominates the others. All are vital, and none should be neglected.

The fourth aspect of the church's ministry is her ministry to herself. There is a legitimate sense in which the church should meet her own needs. She should attend to her own spiritual health and growth.

The church should grow not only numerically or financially but spiritually. Spiritual growth is not easily measured, but discernment should tell us what attitudes prevail among God's people. Is a congregation marked by concern for or by indifference to the needs of men? Is there fellowship, or is there dissention? Are Christians clinging to an inherited cultural Christianity, or are they following Christ in meaningful discipleship? Is the church preoccupied with her own survival or is she attempting to meet the needs of men? Does the church gather together around the Gospel, or is there some other center for the congregation?

Too often what is called the church's growth in spiritual maturity is really only keeping programs operating smoothly. But we should note that some programs do minister to the spiritual growth of the church, such as Bible studies and prayer groups. Worship services also contribute to the growth of Christians, as do various types of training groups.

The church needs many varied kinds of ministry. She should know and conserve her heritage, and she should follow the Spirit's leadership into all truth by exploring new things. When the church is forgetful, she needs reminding, when she is confused, she needs enlightening, when she is uncertain, she needs assurance, when she is afraid, she needs courage, when she is rebellious, she needs repentance, when she is discouraged, she needs God's promises. Always the church needs to be taught to pray, to be exposed to Scripture, to be directed in decisions, and to be challenged to discipleship. Most of all the church needs faith, that profound personal trust that she is not alone and that God is with her always, even in her failure.

Various ways of explaining the mission of the church are available. We have looked at mission in terms of the church's worship of God, her evangelism of and service to the world, and her building up of herself spiritually. In each of these aspects of mission the example was set by Christ. Christ showed the church how to worship; Christ showed the church how to preach to men; Christ showed the church how to meet the needs of men; and Christ nourished the first disciples in their faith. When Christ calls upon the church to minister in these ways, he does not say "Go see if you can do it." He says: "Come and I will help you do it." And he does.

The Ordinances of the Church

The ordinances of the church are baptism and the Lord's Meal. They are called ordinances because Christ ordained them for his church. On the night before his death he instituted the meal saying "This do in remembrance of me" (I Corinthians 11:24-25). Following his resurrection he commissioned his disciples to go into the world preaching and baptizing (Matthew 28:19-20). In obedience to these commands of the Lord the Christian church has practiced baptism and the Lord's Meal without interruption for almost two thousand years.

It is interesting to notice that over these many years different names have been given to the Lord's Meal. It is known as the eucharist which means thanksgiving, as communion, as mass, and as the Lord's supper. All of these words are useful; it does not matter very much which name we use. Most Christians today refer to baptism and the Lord's Meal as sacraments. We elect to call them ordinances because we think that it is very important to remember that Christ ordained them.

The Roman Catholic Church practices seven sacraments, while Protestant churches practice only two. One reason that Protestants have only two is that they believe Christ ordained only two. The five other ceremonies which the Roman Catholic Church practices are confirmation, ordination, marriage, confession, and unction. Protestants practice some of these ceremonies as well as Catholics, but Protestants do not call them ordinances because Christ did not ordain them. For example, Christ blessed marriage, but he did not ordain it since it existed long before he lived upon earth.

There is another reason why baptism and the Lord's Meal have a special place in Christian theology and practice. The church is a Gospel church. The ordinances are Gospel ordinances. Baptism and the Lord's Meal are distinguished clearly from the other ceremonies because both of them preach the Gospel. Just as a pastor may preach about Christ's death and resurrection so that men may hear it, so baptism and the Lord's Meal preach about Christ's death and resurrection so that men may see it. In baptism the entry into the water speaks of Christ's entering into death and burial. Coming from the water speaks of Christ's resurrection. In the meal the pieces of bread speak of Christ's body broken by scourging and thorns, sword and nails, and the wine speaks of Christ's blood which was spilled during his execution. This is a very important thing to say about the ordinances: they preach the Gospel. In them the Gospel is being enacted before the church like a play on a stage.

A great many Christians today do not appreciate the ordinances. They feel that spiritual realities are the only things that matter; external ceremonies are not important. They assume that as we move away from ceremonies we will move closer to the spiritual realities behind them. But this is a mistaken view. The truth, as the church has learned from long experience, is that as we move away from the ceremonies, we also move away from the spiritual realities behind them. The church might long ago have lost or obscured its message, the Gospel, except for external reminders like the ordinances. When God chooses to reveal himself to men, he does not hesitate to use external means. We have seen that when God came among men in history, he came not as an elusive phantom but as a real man. Jesus really was one of us, with a body like other men. Similarly, when the Lord selected means of preaching the Gospel, he chose to use not only the elusive words of various preachers but also tangible objects from this tangible world: water, wine, and bread. The church is to observe these ceremonies because God's people need these physical presentations of the Gospel.

What else can be said about the ordinances? We say that Christ is present in them. He is in the water. He is in the bread and the wine. He is with the church when a new member comes in, and he is with the church when she eats this meal. When he commissioned his disciples to go preaching and baptizing, he promised to be with them always. When he commanded them to observe the meal, he spoke of the elements as his body and blood. Christ is here, in baptism and in the Lord's Meal.

Christ is preached by these ceremonies, and Christ is

present in them. Because Protestants have reacted so strongly against Catholic views of the eucharist as Christ's substantial presence, they often have been reluctant to speak of God's presence and work at all in these ceremonies. That is the case with many Baptists, and *The Baptist Faith and Message* embodies this reluctance. But when we speak only of men's work and do not speak of God's presence and of God's work, then we have missed the most important point. It is not a good defense of our faith to have so little faith that we do not believe that in this water and at this meal the Lord is here as he promised, working through these earthly means to help us.

Evangelical Christians often object that since the Spirit always dwells in every believer, there is nothing special about his presence in the ordinances. This is not so. The Spirit *is* present with individual believers; the Spirit is present with them in a special way when two or three are gathered together in Christ's name. The church congregating is a special thing, special because it is different from an individual Christian by himself. Similarly when the congregation observes baptism or the meal Christ is present with them in a special way, special because these ceremonies are different from a simple congregation. For too long many evangelicals have treated these ordinances from the Lord in a casual and cavalier fashion, little realizing how serious it is to become indifferent to these precious gifts which are so important to the spiritual welfare of God's church. This will end if we accept these gifts with gratitude, learning in faith to see God at work for us in them.

So far what we have said about the ordinances is this: Christ gave the church these ceremonies; they preach the Gospel; Christ is present when they are observed; and God works through them to help the church. Now let us consider baptism and the Lord's Meal separately.

I am a Baptist, and Baptists traditionally have said two distinctive things about baptism, one about its candidates, the other about its mode. Baptists say that baptism is for believers, not for infants; and they say that baptism is to be administered by immersion, not by touching a few drops of water on the forehead. Both of these ideas are controversial. Most of the Christians in the world accept infant baptism performed in ways other than immersion. Let us talk first about the mode of baptism.

Today there is widespread agreement among New Testament scholars that the word "baptizo" refers to immersion, and there is fairly widespread agreement that the mode of baptism in the New Testament was usually if not always immersion. Even so, the argument against immersion goes, the mode is not important. Certainly I would agree that the mode of baptism is not as important as the meaning of baptism. I cannot say that a ceremony using modes other than immersion is not really baptism, for the primary meaning of baptism rests upon what the Lord does, not upon the manner in which men perform the ceremony. As a Baptist I certainly do not feel superior to the many Christians who do not practice baptism by immersion. But in all candor I must add that I am grateful for my Baptist heritage. I am thankful that brave men in the past have stubbornly practiced baptism by immersion in spite of opposition. I treasure this gift of God to us on behalf of all the church, hoping that one day we Baptists may be able to share it with other Christian brothers. We do not esteem immersion so highly because it is beautiful, for it is often an awkward, unsightly ceremony. We esteem it because it speaks so eloquently of the Gospel: Here is a living man, he dies, he is buried, he rises again with a new life. In particular, as theologian Karl Barth has observed,[1] immersion itself constitutes real threat to the life of the candidate, a threat which is very appropriate—he is dying to an old life and beginning a new one. We treasure immersion also because it is a ceremony which Christ underwent at the beginning of his public ministry. It is a precious heritage.

Baptists say that believers are the only proper candidates for baptism. We realize fully that the church has a responsibility to minister to unbelievers of all ages, including infants who are too young to have faith. But we also believe that

[1]See Karl Barth, *The Teaching of the Church Regarding Baptism.*

baptism, properly understood, marks the beginning of Christian discipleship, a discipleship that cannot be had by proxy of parents or godparents, a discipleship that begins when a man encounters the forgiving Christ in profound personal trust. Baptism is a ceremony observed one time, once and for all, signifying that once and for all Christ has forgiven this man and made him to be God's son. Baptism is the doorway into the invisible church because it is a visible sign of an invisible reality that has occurred in the life of a believer.

The ordinances speak of two aspects of the church's experience of salvation. Baptism speaks of the once-for-all aspect of salvation called conversion, and the meal speaks of the continuing aspect of salvation called sanctification. We are baptized once and for all; we eat the Lord's Meal many times. We are thankful for the Baptist heritage which points to this inner experience of salvation, as well as pointing to the Gospel events which made this experience possible. That is why we believe that, ideally, baptism is the immersion of a believer.

Earlier we mentioned that evangelical Christians reject the view that baptism is essential to salvation. When the word salvation refers to the once-for-all forgiveness and justification of the man who accepts Christ, it is clearly a work of grace based upon Christ's sacrifice and given to an individual not because he merits it but simply because God loves him (see Chapter Eight). Baptism has nothing to do with this, except that it is the man's public confession that he has been converted. But if "salvation" is used in a wider sense to include all that God does over a period of time to change the believer into the likeness of Christ, then baptism does contribute to it, just as sermons, Bible-reading, the Lord's Meal, and prayers contribute to it. Since it is natural to think of the once-for-all aspect of salvation in connection with baptism, it is misleading to speak of "baptismal regeneration" or to say that it is necessary to be baptized in order to be saved.

Now let us consider the Lord's Meal. We said that baptism

speaks of the inner conversion of an individual by which he begins his life as a Christian. The Lord's Meal speaks of the inner sanctification of an individual by which he continues his life as a Christian, and thus the meal is eaten repeatedly.

In the past there have been two problems about the Lord's Meal. One is whether it is a sacrifice. The other is how we are to understand Christ's real presence at the meal. We may speak very briefly of each one.

The problem of the sacrifice sharply divides Catholics and Protestants. The division is illustrated by the fact that in Catholic church buildings there are altars while in Protestant church buildings there are tables. Protestants do not think of themselves as offering a sacrifice but as eating a meal. They may say that the meal is an appropriate time for all Christians to present their bodies as living sacrifices, or they may say that the meal symbolizes the sacrifice of Christ, but Protestants would never say that in the meal a priest somehow offers up Christ to God the Father. But do Catholics say this? In the past the Roman Catholic Church has said this, and by its official statements apparently it is committed to this today. But according to the learned scholar E. L. Mascall, among Roman Catholic theologians today there is an "almost universal refusal to admit that *the Mass* either repeats or supplements the sacrifice of Christ."[1] If this is true, it is an important development; at any rate it encourages us to look elsewhere for our understanding of the meaning of the meal.

There is widespread disagreement among Christians about the manner in which Christ is present at the meal. In the past Roman Catholics have affirmed that the substance of the bread (its essential bread-ness) was changed into the substance of Christ, though the accidents of the bread (its taste, size, color) remained unchanged. Martin Luther, the great sixteenth century reformer, rejected the view that the elements are transformed into Christ's body. He said instead

[1]E. L. Mascall, "Eucharist, Eucharistic Theology," in *A Dictionary of Christian Theology*, ed. Alan Richardson.

that there is no change, but that Christ is simply present "in; with, and under" the substance of the bread and wine. Other more radical reformers went so far as to deny that Christ is present at all in the meal. They said that the meal is a human ceremony symbolizing what Christ has done by his sacrifice. This cannot be the whole story, for surely Christ is present with his church always, and so he is present with her when she eats the meal. What really concerns Christians is not the presence of Christ as a substance but his presence as a Savior, Lord, and friend. There is a famous sentence from a book by Phillip Melanchthon, a friend of Martin Luther. He wrote, "To know Christ is to know his benefits, not the manner of his incarnation."[1] Similarly we might say of the meal, "To know Christ in this meal is to know his benefits, not the manner of his presence." What really matters is that Christ is here joining the church in this meal. He is an unseen host sharing food for our spirits by giving his love, direction, and encouragement to us. There is nothing magical or superstitious about Christ's presence at the meal, but there is something profoundly spiritual and serious about it.

Let us summarize what we have said about the ordinances. The Gospel ordinances are essential to the Gospel church. Christ ordained that the church should observe them for her spiritual welfare. He comes to the church and ministers to her through the ordinances. The ordinances show the Gospel to men's eyes as preaching puts it in men's ears. Baptism symbolizes the finished salvation of the church and the meal symbolizes her continuing growth as God graciously feeds her. The ordinances are gifts to be treasured and shared in the Christian church.

Some of the issues which I have raised here are rarely discussed in some evangelical circles. I myself was taught as a youth that Christian faith is basically a private matter and that the only necessary ingredients to Christian living are private prayer, private Bible reading, and individual witness-

[1]Phillip Melanchthon, *Loci Communes Theologici,* in the Dedicatory Letter.

ing. In time I have come to think that, though these matters are very important, they are only one part of the story of Christian living and of Christian faith. Christian faith and life are essentially social. God has planned the church for the welfare of Christians. The church is God's people, Christ's body, the Spirit's fellowship. Local congregations hold an important place in the purposes of God. The entire church has been called to be a community of worship, witness, service, and spiritual growth. The Lord has given to the church the ordinances for her welfare. This may not be the way you and I would have done things, but I believe that it is the way God has done them. Let us pray that we may come to see the church as God sees her.

For further reading:

For the biblical data see Paul Minear, *Images of the Church in the New Testament*. Two creative theological studies are Claude Welch, *The Reality of the Church* and F. W. Dillistone, *The Structure of the Divine Society*. Baptist views may be surveyed in W. S. Hudson, ed., *Baptist Concepts of the Church*; for a down-to-earth Baptist statement see E. Glenn Hinson, *The Church: Design for Survival*. On the meal Fred Howard's *Interpreting the Lord's Supper* is good.

11. CHRISTIAN HOPE

Is Hope Healthy?

A few years ago anyone who spoke of hope and of the future had to defend himself against accusations that he was an idle dreamer or worse. Christians were accused of promising to working people "a pie in the sky when you die" with the result that people would not try to rectify the social and economic sins of the world.

Sometimes Christians were guilty of these charges. They were so heavenly minded that they were no earthly good. In spite of the angel's admonition, "Why stand ye gazing up into heaven?" (Acts 1:11), they talked about the end of the world so much that they did not have the time or energy left to do anything about the world they lived in. They told dreadful deathbed stories that revealed nothing so vividly as the inability of the storyteller to minister to dying persons. They sometimes wore sandwich boards proclaiming the immediate end of the world, in spite of Jesus' instructions that the time of the end was none of our business (see Acts 1:7).

Recently there has been a change in attitude toward the doctrine of hope. Many men now recognize that it is reasonable to give some attention to questions about the future. Future talk is not being consigned to fanatics. Many Americans now candidly confess that for years we have tried to ignore the stark reality of death and that our repression of feelings and thoughts about death borders on the neurotic. We now see that it is possible to view the future of life on the planet without indulging in apocalyptic pessimism or starry-eyed utopianism. In brief, it is now recognized that we can be realistic about the future.

Christians have a built-in concern for the future. The historical character of the Christian religion has always given us a forward-looking dimension. Israel always looked forward to Messiah; Christians have always looked forward to the return of Messiah. Furthermore, Christians believe that through Jesus and his resurrection there is a word of hope to be said even in the face of the most grim enemy of man, death. Only when Christians have been overwhelmed by what we now recognize to be the sentimental spirit of the modern age have they failed to speak of hope. Now that is all past and hope can once again be restored to its place of importance alongside faith and love as the great Christian virtues (I Corinthians 13:13).

Albert Schweitzer said that one of the most important issues faced by a religion is whether it is life-affirming or life-denying. Though despair for the present life has sometimes led Christians to be life-denying and to retreat into escapist longings for the future, this is not the only position open to a Christian. Christianity is a life-affirming religion. We believe that God created this world, that God loves this world, that God wants us to be in this world (though not of it). We believe, in fact, that God came into this world, thus affirming his continued concern about this world. So we affirm our present lives. We feel that by God's grace we have our families, our work, our friends, our ministries, our nation, our food. We love this world, and our interest in another more lasting world does not detract from our love for this one. In fact, it enhances it. Just because we have hope for an eternal life, we can also have a great appreciation for this life.

Hope is an important ingredient for any healthy life. In fact, it may be indispensable. It may be that human beings are created so that they cannot live without hope. Unless there is something to look forward to in the future, they may become unable to live in the present. So hope may be not just healthy; it may be essential to human health.

One of the saddest descriptions of the man without Christ is found in Ephesians 2:11-12. It concludes: "without hope and without God." From a Christian perspective, a man without God is a man without hope, ultimately. We may have short-range hopes (for better pay or passing an exam or getting married) but there cannot be an ultimate hope without God.

The Christian sees God as standing in the future, calling out to us to continue on our journey. He awaits our response. The future is God's: God draws us toward himself as we live toward the future. God makes promises which will be fulfilled in the future. God is not a relic confined to the past or merely a dimension of our present experience: God is the one toward whom we move as we move toward the future.

The New Testament provides us with many materials for our understanding of the future. Christians are divided over how to understand the New Testament on this matter, and the debates about eschatology (last things) are complicated. This is especially true of the often-used word "kingdom." Jesus often preached and told parables about the kingdom, but what did he mean? The traditional position was that Jesus was predicting some characteristics of a future domain of God on earth. Liberal Protestants thought that we Christians should set up the kingdom of God now by establishing social equality and economic justice. Albert Schweitzer thought that Jesus was preaching that the end of the world had come and that Jesus was mistaken and so died in despair; Schweitzer's position is called "thoroughgoing eschatology." In reaction to this extreme view, C. H. Dodd and others have said that the kingdom was present in Jesus: this means that the kingdom came in the proclamation of Jesus. This view, called "realized eschatology," made much of phrases like "the kingdom of God is within you" (Luke 17:21).

It is not, in my judgment, necessary for us to make a

decision about these technical matters in order to speak meaningfully of Christian hope. Rather, we can try to isolate the issues which are important to us as we think of our hope. Then it will not matter what "kingdom" is thought to refer to, for we will have plenty of material for our reflections.

The first item we must consider is the resurrection of Christ, apart from which there would not be a Christian religion at all, let alone a Christian hope. Then we must speak on the unpleasant subject of our own death and of our hope for resurrection. Next we shall speak of the end of history ("the day of Christ"), and finally we shall talk of the two dimensions of eternity, heaven and hell.

Easter

In America today Easter is often treated as a nature festival, complete with bunnies, eggs, flowers, and spring weather. But Easter is not a nature festival; it is a history festival. It is the celebration of the event which climaxed the life and ministry of Jesus Christ. It is a time for rejoicing about his resurrection from death.

As part of the Gospel, the resurrection of Christ is very important for the Christian faith. Yet, oddly, it is not often understood very well. Theologian Reinhold Niebuhr has described accurately the inadequacies in Christian preaching about Easter.[1] Conservative Christians tend to stress the factuality of Christ's resurrection. With great learning and much effort they argue that this story is firmly rooted in history. They support their argument with many varied New Testament texts which report the event. They supplement the texts with well-reasoned logic. They ask, for example, who could be responsible for the disappearance of Christ's body from the grave, pointing out that the enemies of Christ would hardly have stolen it. And his friends, who might have done so, would surely not have died (as many did) for affirming his resurrection had they known it to be a fraud.

In my judgment the historical evidence for the resurrection

[1]See *Applied Christianity*, pp. 52-56.

is very strong. I believe that early Christians came to faith in Christ because of his resurrection. I expect that they wanted sceptics to check their stories; that, at least, would seem to me to be involved in the proclamation of Peter at Pentecost and in the early Christian preaching generally.

Some critics have pointed out difficulties in the New Testament witness to the resurrection. They note the difficulty of reconciling the different Easter morning appearances. I regard this as testimony to the existence of several good traditions; I think it strengthens the case. Critics also note Paul's concern for a spiritual body in resurrection and his report that Jesus appeared to the disciples in much the same way that he appeared to Paul (even the most conservative scholars admit that the appearance to Paul was a vision) (see I Corinthians 15:4-8, 42-44). My response to this is that while there are ambiguities about the method of the resurrection there is clarity about the fact. The early church did not try to explain too much. They did not say that anyone was present at the moment of resurrection. They reported the change in Christ's appearance (if they were making up the story or making adjustments to it, they almost certainly would have omitted this). They did not get together on the sequence of his appearances. The story, in brief, is convincing because it is artless.

Yet Christian preaching that stops with a defense of resurrection, or even after a defense of Christian faith based on the resurrection, is inadequate.

Less conservative Christians attempt to remove from Christian preaching elements which cause embarrassment to secular minds. Among those elements none is more troublesome than the miracles of the Bible, especially the resurrection. So the resurrection is said to be a myth, not history. It is a symbol which speaks of the fact that Jesus' message of brotherhood and love cannot die, cannot be stopped, must be victorious. Although this view is notoriously unbiblical, that is not its only fault. For, like the conservative defense, it fails to speak of the meaning of the resurrection.

The resurrection of Jesus is the decisive stamp of approval on Jesus' life and work. It is the divine "well done" which confirms that Jesus is all that he claimed to be. It is the validation that life and forgiveness are in him and men may hope in him with confidence.

His resurrection is the death of death. It is a promise to us who are finite and sinful that life, not death, is the ultimate reality. It is the word of life spoken to dying men, and there is no other. To whom shall we go? He who is risen has the words of eternal life (see John 6:66-69).

Our Death and Resurrection

In America today not much is said about death. We try to pretend that death is not a reality. We disguise our references to it with euphemisms like "passed away" (died), "the loved one" (the corpse), "memorial service" (the funeral), and "perpetual care family plots" (the cemetery). We dress corpses and pay cosmeticians to make them look "as natural as life." Then we bury them in expensive, ornate containers.

All of this indicates that we are trying to force thoughts about death out of our minds. We cannot face our fear of death, so we repress it from our consciousness. I expect that it comes to the surface as worry about other things, or even as worry about nothing in particular. In any case, we can hardly be said to be facing reality.

The same is true about dying. Many patients ask not to be told that they are terminally ill, and many doctors do not tell them. Families who know the true situation may pretend to the patient that they do not. Patients who learn the truth may find no one with enough compassion and courage to discuss death in a serious and helpful way.

I hope that this bad situation is getting better. Many Christians now are trying to be more realistic about death. Elisabeth Kubler-Ross's book *On Death and Dying* has enabled many ministers and others to minister more effectively to those who are dying. Evelyn Waugh's satire, *The Loved One*, has pointed up the fatuousness of our burial practices. We need to recover our balance on these matters and to learn to think realistically and to minister with compassion and hope in the presence of dying and death.

Death has two different faces for the Christian. It is both natural and terrifying. It is natural in the sense that it is part of nature. All living organisms have a limited life expectancy. Life insurance actuarial charts deal with the statistics and probabilities of death. Man is finite; there is a limit to how long he can live. There have been myths to conceal this—the fountain of youth, the transmigration of the soul, the freezing of one who dies—but it is still clear to anyone who thinks about it that, as we now are, we cannot live forever.

The other face of death is that which confronts man, not as an animal, but as a sinner. Death frightens us. We dread it. Our guilt seems infinite as we face the possibility of judgment. We feel that we are being mistreated. We resent death because it seems to mark the end of all that is worthwhile about life. It is too final, too futile. It is the loss of all hope.

It may well be that we would not fear death if we were not sinners. We might see it only as natural, as other animals apparently see it. But for sinners death is an enemy. It is no friend in disguise but a grim and vicious enemy, and the only response that could be appropriate to it would be to destroy it.

The Christian believes that Jesus did just that by his resurrection. Our hope for resurrection rests on his resurrection. If God raised Jesus, may he not raise us also? While the Christian hope for resurrection may find some support in Pharisaic views of resurrection, and perhaps even in non-Jewish teachings about immortality or in intimations of immortality in nature, the real foundation for Christian hope is Christ's resurrection.

Our hope rests also on our life in the Spirit. The experience we have now of sharing in the divine life encourages us to hope that death will not end this shared life. Our life is "eternal" precisely because it was God's life before it became ours.

Because of an event in the past (the resurrection of Christ) and an experience in the present (life in the Spirit) we have hope for the future (our resurrection). That is the well-founded hope of the Christian.

There are many questions about our resurrection which we cannot answer. The Bible does not give us the data for answering them, and there is no other source. Seances and other alleged communications with the dead do not help. We cannot tell exactly what the relationship is between the molecules of our physical bodies and the components of our resurrected spiritual bodies. We do not know about the age or appearance of our resurrected bodies, and there is no way we can know. We do not know the time of our resurrection, or our status after death and before the time of our resurrection. But these questions about physical matters are secondary to the great issue of whether or not we can hope for a fully personal life after death, and the Christian affirmation of that hope satisfies us when we reflect on it.

Christ's Day

When we think of the future, we think not only of our individual lives, but of human existence on this planet. Mankind is finite just as each man is; there is a limit to mankind's existence. Human life may cease on our planet when the sun burns out. It may end with a nuclear war. God may bring it to an end by a supernatural intervention. In any case, there will not always be people alive on the planet.

We do not know how long people will be living on earth. It may be for thousands of years, or even millions. It may be for only a few years, or less. It is no longer necessary to believe in God in order to recognize the tenuousness of life on our planet. There are plenty of secular doomsday prophets. Recently we have begun to wonder whether we have poisoned nature so irremediably that it will some day be unable to support life any longer. Before that we felt that the production of food could not keep up with the population explosion. Before that we faced the possibility of nuclear war ending all life on the planet. In a perfectly secular sense we are at any moment about twenty minutes away from an event (nuclear war) which would kill virtually everything on earth.

Christians who try to predict the time of the end are out of step with Jesus' statement that we cannot know the time (Acts 1:7). We do not know the time, and we do not need to know it. All that we need to know about the time is that it could be soon or it could be very distant.

How do we live, if we recognize that the time of the end is unknown to us? In some ways we live as if it will not come for a million years. We make plans, we buy insurance, we build houses and schools and hospitals and churches, we cultivate friendships, we plant gardens and orchards and flowers, we try to improve our society, we work for economic justice and mercy, we strive to change the world.

Sometimes we get mixed up and think that the only spiritual behavior is to act as if the end were coming today. But that is untrue. The only spiritual behavior is to act as if the end might be a million years *or* it might be today, for that is our true situation and apparently the situation in which God wants us, since he, though he knows, has not told us, when the end will come.

Many Christians are very concerned about what will happen at the end of the world. There are strong feelings about this question and several definite positions are held. These rotate around the question of a millennium or thousand years reign of Christ (see Revelation 20:1-10).

One position, called amillennialism, holds that Biblical language about Christ reigning on earth for a thousand years is symbolic not literal. The two alternative views say that Christ will rule on earth for a thousand years.

One groups says that the millennium will be preceded by Christ's coming to save all Christians from seven years of tribulation which will precede the millennium. Known as premillennialism, this view places much emphasis on I Thessalonians 4.

Post-millennialists hold that the thousand year reign will be constituted by men improving their world so much that Christ is Lord, though Christ will not literally be present on earth. This view is not very popular now because the twentieth century has been so barbaric that it is difficult to believe that society is progressing toward a golden age of peace under the rule of God.

Baptists have traditionally been amillennial. I do not know of any major Baptist Confession which is premillennial or postmillennial. There are many Bible texts that can be called upon to support the premillennial view, but these must be pieced together in a manner that seems highly arbitrary to many Christians. The popularity of the premillennial view among Baptists today is to be attributed to the influence of the Scofield Reference Bible and other dispensational writings. Few Baptists are even aware that dispensationalism is a new and novel way of understanding the Bible and that it is out of touch with older Baptist traditions.

The important question about the end is not "When?" or "How?" but "Who?" Who will be in control? Who will be in charge? To this question the Christian faith gives a clear answer: the end is the day of Jesus Christ. When we know this fact, we know all that is necessary for our spiritual welfare and our theological understanding. This fact is so important that it overshadows the matters of time and method.

How shall we face the end of life on our planet? If we are Christians, we see it as the fulfillment of the will of him who loves us. If we are not Christians, we see it as the thwarting of our purposes by him whom we do not love. A Christian welcomes the day of Christ, and a non-Christian fears it. For it will be the same Christ then with whom we deal now, and our feeling about the end should be the same as our feelings about Christ now. The future holds what the present holds—Jesus Christ.

Hell

The Bible contains some vivid pictures of the destiny of men who reject God, including the teaching of Jesus who likened hell to the garbage dump of Jerusalem "where the worms don't die and the fire never goes out" (Mark 9:43-48). In the Middle Ages these pictures were given great attention. They were treated literally, enlarged on generously, and eventually elevated to a primary place in orthodox teaching and evangelistic preaching, in spite of the fact that in the New Testament they never held such a place, as we can see by observing the records of the Gospel proclamation in Acts and elsewhere.

Traditionally there have been four views about hell. One is that it is an eternal separation from God which is an existence of torment and pain. The strength of this view is that it takes the Bible teaching about sin and judgment very seriously. Its weakness is that it is not able to attribute a final victory to God. The God who loves men seems to have failed to win victory over all evil. Unless we return to a double-edged predestination which affirms that God demonstrates his majesty by pre-determining that some persons will go to hell, then God's majesty is not affirmed by this view. But to most people's moral sensitivities predestination in this sense is untenable, which is why it is rejected by most evangelical Christians today.

A second view is that there is no hell and all men will be saved. Called universalism, its chief strength is that it affirms the ultimate victory of God's love. Its weakness is that it seems to say that God does not respect human freedom, since everyone goes to heaven no matter what decisions he makes. It has almost no support in the Bible.

A third view is annihilationism. It teaches that those who finally resist God simply cease to exist as persons. Its strength is that it is a merciful view which nevertheless portrays God as respecting human decisions. Its weakness is that it finds only meager support in the Bible; for example, it regards the biblical references to destruction (as in Matthew 10:28) as literal. Its real support comes from a Platonic view of existence: the good is real, evil is non-existent. It also fails to show how, if men cease to exist, God's love for them is finally triumphant.

Finally, there is the position that hell is real but not eternal. It is therefore, in reality, simply purgatory. The strength of this view is that it both takes the judgment of God seriously and shows his grace as ultimately triumphant for all men. Its disadvantages are that it seems to be out of step with some biblical passages in which hell is pictured as endless. Also, what reason is there to suppose that, even in hell, all men will eventually come to accept God? There is no evidence for this in the Bible, and I cannot see any evidence for it in the lives of men on earth. As Jesus said, the way to hell is broad and crowded; this is not because God wants it that way but because, as a matter of fact, that is what men choose.

Perhaps no one of these views is entirely correct. I, at least, do not find any one entirely convincing. Instead of choosing one of them, I prefer to list what I believe to be the principles which should govern our understanding of hell.

First—and most important for us today—God is going to do what is right. As we saw in Chapter Three, this principle rests upon the revelation of God's righteousness given to the seventh century prophets and climaxed in Jesus. God does right. We cannot overestimate the importance of that principle.

That principle is more important than the fact that people are going to hell. I am more concerned to say that God does right than I am that people are going to hell, for if God does not do right, then we are all going to hell—in fact we are there already. The only hope men have rests upon the righteousness of God, for if God does not do right, by definition there can be no heaven; all is hell.

When people are troubled by what they hear about hell, I am much more concerned to testify to God's doing right than I am to any details about hell. Unless they know he will do right they cannot possibly become Christians, for to trust in an unrighteous God would be to trust in an idol. The only real God is righteous.

Once we seriously believe in God's righteousness then we are able to move on to a second principle about hell. The second principle is this: God respects our decisions. He loves us, but he does not force his love on us. To force love is to commit assault, which means that it reveals what seemed to be love was only uncontrollable lust, not love at all. Just because he loves us he does not make us accept him and his love. He allows us to decide. He loves us, he encourages our response, he woos us, he pursues us, he urges us, but he does not force us, because he respects us.

The third item about hell is a statement of fact, not a principle. The fact is that men reject God. They do so repeatedly, frequently, in many ways. They do so finally, with determination. That, at least, is the effect of the lives of most men, even if it is not always their intention. Jesus observed this in his own day, and, it seems to me, we can observe it clearly today. By and large people do not seem to be interested in knowing and loving God or each other, or, for that matter, in loving themselves. Life is wasted with things which do not matter while things that do matter are neglected or even rejected. Many never suspect what their lives might have been.

This brings us to our final comment about hell, namely, that it may be described as God's letting us go in order that we may do what we want to do. We see this in the phrase "God gave them up" in Romans (1:24, 26, 28). Several years ago a television show told the story of a fictional bank robber who was shot to death by the police. He was "raised" by a man in a white suit who said that he was the robber's guardian angel. "I am here to give you whatever you want," he said. He took the robber to a large apartment with elegant furniture, a well-stocked bar, stereophonic music, and several beautiful girls. The robber was delighted at first, but he soon became bored and asked to be taken to a pool hall. His request was granted, and he was elated when with his first shot he sank all the balls into the pockets. Soon he tired of this too, and he told the angel he wanted to rob a bank. The angel arranged this, and the robbery went off without a hitch, the robber escaping with several sacks of money. He repeated this activity several times, until once more he became bored and miserable. but when the angel asked what he wanted, the robber could not think of anything to ask for. The story closed with dialogue like this:

> "Well, Angel, I'd better tell you something. You see, there's been a mistake. On earth I was a bad guy, see? So I really belong in hell with the other bad guys, see? I mean, I don't really deserve to be here in heaven, you understand? So send me away from heaven."
> "My friend, you have made a mistake. Whatever made you think this is heaven?"

That is the really tragic side of our life, that if we insist on having our own way, we are certain to create a hell for ourselves. That is why C. S. Lewis once remarked that there are two kinds of people, those who say to God "Your will be done" and those to whom God finally must say, "Your will be done." While we may be sure that God will employ every means to bring men to himself because he cares for them, still Scripture and experience teach us that some people refuse to be brought to God. The tragic truth is that there will come a point at which there remains no option open to God but to "give them up."

Heaven

The Bible gives us many dramatic descriptions of the destiny of God's children, the longest of which is the "heavenly Jerusalem" of Revelation 21 and 22. In that passage heaven is described as a real and wonderful place.

We today have failed to grasp either the reality or the wonder of heaven. We properly reject the idea that it could be located on a geographer's map or an astronomer's chart, but we do not go on to ask if there really is a destiny for

God's people. This failure to go on is a *de facto* capitulation to skepticism, and it leads to enormous frustration. The novelist John Updike has recorded this frustration vividly in a story entitled "Pigeon Feathers." He tells of a young boy who visited a new church while he was staying with his grandparents. The boy discovered, to his amazement, that the minister of the church did not believe in a real heaven. He told his mother about this incredible fact, only to learn that she too did not really believe. The boy was left wondering what there is to believe in if heaven is a mistake. He was not the first to feel that way, for Paul long ago wrote: "If it is for this life only that Christ has given us hope, we of all men are most to be pitied" (I Corinthians 15:19).

We communicate our uncertainty about heaven in various ways, one of which is to picture it as a place of fluffy white clouds. That insubstantial picture is in sharp contrast to the solidity of the city with twelve foundations and streets hard as glass in Revelation 21.

Heaven is also pictured in the Bible as wonderful, and we likewise fail to express that. In contrast to the darkness of night in the first century John says heaven is always lighted. In contrast to unchecked disease John says heaven has trees whose leaves heal all sickness. In contrast to the parched desert of Israel John says that heaven has an endless river of crystal-clear water. In contrast to a meagre existence John says heaven has trees with twelve kinds of fruits growing on them. In brief, John makes every effort to describe heaven as a wonderful destiny.

We have not done this in our day. People today do not want to go to heaven. At football games our cheerleaders say to their opponents, "Go to Hell, State University" but they never say, "Go to heaven, Home Team." In our attempt to be profoundly thoughtful we became foolishly cynical, and we capitulate to the current prejudice against the idea that God might finish the work he has begun.

We have not spoken to our contemporaries as the Bible spoke to the first century. We often hear people say that heaven sounds boring: "I don't want to stand around all day strumming a harp." A moment's reflection on the variety of our physical universe should reassure us that God is not likely to create a boring destiny for us. John's musical images might mean more to today's youth if we visualize people in heaven wearing blue jeans and strumming guitars. Surely the point John wanted to make was that a noble human activity—music —has its place and its fulfillment in heaven in the praise of God.

In heaven people will be good. Heaven is the third phase of salvation. The first phase was the point at which our sins were forgiven; the second phase is the process of God working in our lives to change us; the third phase is the completion of this process, in heaven. Traditionally this phase has been called glorification, and to it Paul referred when he wrote: "The One who started the good work in you will bring it to completion by the Day of Christ Jesus" (Philippians 1:6).

For me, this is the most difficult thing to believe about the Christian faith, that God can make us into really good people. I find this much harder to understand than I do miracles or other customary difficulties. How can God make us really good? It cannot be by magic; it must be moral, for we are persons not puppets. By what activity of God can we come to love God with all our hearts and to love others as we do ourselves? How can we be transformed into the image of Jesus, the obedient and self-sacrificing Son? I do not understand how God can do it, but it is my hope that he can. This is one case in which we trust him for what seems to us to be an almost impossible task.

We do have some idea about what he is doing. For one thing, we have an experience of what it is to be good in some areas. Let us imagine a hypothetical situation in which I had a pistol in my hand and a friend were sitting in front of me. Can I shoot a friend or not? I know how to aim a pistol and to pull the trigger; in that sense I can shoot him. But in another sense I cannot shoot him, for I am not capable of killing a friend. It does not matter whether you call this freedom or the absence of freedom. The point is: I am the kind of person who cannot shoot a friend.

When we speak of being good persons in heaven, we mean that we will become the *kinds* of persons who love God and one another. We will be free to love because we will be that kind of persons—lovers.

What does God do to make this possible? He brings us into the circle of his love. He loves us and so we learn to love in return. I do not understand all of it, but I hope sincerely that somehow he will be able to finish the work of transforming us all into lovers of him and of one another.

There is more to be said about heaven. In heaven men live together in community. God has always been concerned about a people, Israel in the Old Testament and the church in the New Testament. Heaven will be the fulfillment of his purpose to create a people for himself. And that means that there we shall live together in friendship, in *koinonia*.

People often ask if we shall know each other in heaven. The Dutch theologian Noordmann responds: Do we know each other now?[1] That is the point. Right now we live in isolation from each other, even in crowds. Only in rare moments do we experience intimacy, and those moments are the best in our lives. They are also a promise of what is to be our destiny when we live together in unhindered friendship with one another. Right now we are kept apart from one another by our sin and guilt and by how we feel about ourselves; when we become good persons then it will follow naturally that we can have love for one another.

But the most important thing to be said about heaven is not its reality and wonder, and not its good people living in fellowship. The most important thing is that in heaven we shall see God face to face (see Revelation 22:4). Jesus spoke of this in the beatitude: "How blest are those whose hearts are pure; they shall see God" (Matthew 5:8). Paul also spoke of it: "Now we see only puzzling reflections in a mirror, but then we shall see face to face. My knowledge now is partial; then it

[1]Quoted in Hendrikus Berkhof, *Well-Founded Hope*, Chapter 9.

will be whole, like God's knowledge of me" (I Corinthians 13:12).

In the Bible God's communication with men on earth is spoken of in terms of "speaking and hearing." Heaven is spoken of in terms of seeing and being seen. So the church traditionally has described heaven as the "beatific vision," the blessed vision of God.

Augustine long ago described man's need for God in these famous words:

> "Lord, thou has made us for thyself and our hearts are restless until they find their rest in thee."
>
> (*Confessions*, I, 1)

God begins to calm our restlessness when we first come to know him, but we continue to experience a sense of incompleteness, a sense that we somehow still lack something. What we lack is the ultimate presence of God which is possible only when we see him face to face.

There are many mysteries which trouble us now. The most difficult of these is the existence of evil. In heaven, when evil has been destroyed (not explained), when we are good persons, when we see the fulfillment of God's ultimate purpose to create a society of free men who live together in love of God and in love of one another, then we shall "understand" how God is just. One aspect of the vision of God will be a theodicy, an understanding of the righteousness of God in his dealings with men. This will complete the revelation of his goodness which began with the Hebrew prophets and reached its historical climax in the victorious sacrifice of Christ.

In this book we have followed the procedure of thinking about God, and we have now reflected on the ultimate possible experience for a man, namely, an undistorted vision of God. But there is one further word to be said about God. We have discussed his revelation of himself as Father, Son, and Spirit, but we have not yet attempted to combine what we said about each of these into one understanding of God. To do that is to make a statement about the Trinity, and that is the purpose of the final chapter of this book.

For further reading:

I recommend Hendrikus Berkhof's *Well-Founded Hope* as an introduction to eschatology. A. M. Ramsey's *On the Resurrection of Christ* is short but seems to me to say what is needed. I have already mentioned Elisabeth Kubler-Ross's *On Death and Dying*. In various books P. T. Forsyth stressed the moral necessity of judgment: see S. J. Mikolaski, ed., *The Creative Theology of P. T. Forsyth*, especially Chapter Seven. On the theology of hope see Jurgen Moltmann's book by that name, especially the opening "Meditation on Hope." A Baptist presentation from a biblical perspective is Ray Summer's *The Life Beyond*. C. S. Lewis is very helpful about hell and heaven; see *The Great Divorce*.

12. FATHER, SON, AND HOLY SPIRIT

Introduction

The most distinctive thing that Christians say about God is that he is Father, Son, and Holy Spirit. In saying this we do not feel any kinship with other religions which happen to have a sort of divine trinity, for the Christian concern is not for threeness in itself. Nor do Christians have any interest in threenesses in nature like spring-river-lake or in thought like past-present-future.

Nor is the Christian doctrine of the Trinity a sort of patchwork quilt put together by combining snippets of Scripture in an arbitrary way. Some theologians have said that the data for the doctrine of the Trinity are biblical texts which mention the three persons (for example, Matthew 28:19-20, II Corinthians 13:14), together with texts which refer to the deity of the Son and of the Spirit.[1]

It is my judgment that this view is mistaken. The doctrine of the Trinity is not about bits and pieces of the Bible: it is about God. Further, it is perilous to say that the Trinity rests on scattered texts, for the thoughtful student soon realizes that the texts cannot support all the weight of this doctrine. As a result, some persons who are really Christian in sentiment begin to express doubts about the Trinity while others who do not wish to be unorthodox remain silent but insecure about this strange understanding of God. Both groups plead: "This is a mystery we can never grasp," but

[1]See Dallas Roark, *The Christian Faith*, pp. 106-107.

what they really mean is "I am afraid of this, so let us not talk about it." However reverent it may sound to plead that this is a mystery, it is certainly not virtuous to be this insecure about what purports to be the distinctive Christian teaching about God.

This insecurity is very obvious in *The Baptist Faith and Message*, which speaks of God under the three headings (God the Father, God the Son, God the Holy Spirit) but does not attempt to relate them. *The Baptist Faith and Message* is supposed to be consensus theology, and its silence is unfortunately an accurate representation of the Southern Baptist consensus. I believe that we should break this silence. I think this can be done if we re-examine the revelation which God has given to us.

The Revelation of the Trinity

Let us begin with a frank confession: the New Testament does not teach the doctrine of the Trinity. This doctrine has been developed over the years in response to needs in the church. Early Christian confessions, like the Apostles' Creed, were tripartite (divided according to Father, Son, and Spirit), so the movement toward a doctrine of the Trinity is very early. But self-conscious discussion of the subject came only with the rejection of heresies like Sabellianism (third century) and the writing of books like *On Not Three Gods* (Gregory of Nyssa, fourth century), and *On the Trinity* (Augustine, fifth century). These books were motivated by difficulties which the church faced as it confessed more and more explicitly the deity of Christ (at Nicea, 325 A.D.) and of the Spirit (at Constantinople, 381 A.D.).

In the New Testament there are discussions of various doctrines. For example, sin is discussed (Romans 1-2), as is the person of Christ (John 1:1-14), and justification by grace (Galatians and Romans). There is not a corresponding discussion of the Trinity. In that sense, then, does the doctrine of the Trinity have a biblical foundation?

It is this: the Bible testifies to the facts for which the

doctrine of the Trinity attempts to give an account. The Bible speaks of the fact of the God of Israel and Father of Jesus Christ; it speaks of the fact of Jesus of Nazareth; it speaks of the fact of the Spirit who came to the church at Pentecost. The doctrine of the Trinity is a statement about the reality of the God who called Israel, who was incarnate as Jesus, and who now lives in Christians as the Spirit. So the data for the doctrine of the Trinity are not scattered texts; the data are the facts mentioned above, to which the texts refer.

The facts for which the doctrine of the Trinity attempts to account are living facts. As theologian Leonard Hodgson has pointed out, the early Christians practiced trinitarian religion before they developed a trinitarian theology.[1] They said things about the deity of Jesus and the Spirit; they prayed to God in Jesus' name; they described their experience as life "in the Spirit." All of these experiences called for a revision of the understanding of God which they had inherited from their Jewish forefathers. Furthermore, they said that Jesus prayed to the Father, that the Spirit directed and empowered Jesus, and that the Father sent the Spirit.

I have called attention to three facts about the doctrine of the Trinity. First, it is a doctrine about God. Second, it is an attempt by monotheists to account for Jesus and the Spirit. Third, it is closely related to the distinctly Christian experience of God. From this we see clearly that it certainly is not an abstraction.

Analogies of the Trinity

When we first spoke about God (Chapter Three) we observed that the most important thing to be said is that God is personal. If we follow that principle when we attempt to find analogies for the doctrine of the Trinity, we shall avoid the use of impersonal analogies. The Christian habit of speaking about ice/steam/water or the three sides of a triangle is precluded when we realize that, when we are

[1]Leonard Hodgson, *The Doctrine of the Trinity; How Can God be Both One and Three?* "The Glory of the Eternal Trinity," *Christianity Today*, May 25, 1962.

speaking about God, personal analogies are superior to impersonal ones.

If we use personal analogies, only two options are open to us. We may speak of God as one person and then try to understand his threeness in terms of the various activities of one person (like feeling, thinking, and deciding). This analogy is known as the psychological analogy.

The other personal analogy we may use is that of three persons (like Tom, Dick, and Harry). This is the social analogy. If we use it then we must try to understand the unity of the three persons in terms of their purposes or actions or character, or something of the sort.

Each analogy has received support in the past. Gregory of Nyssa used the social analogy in the fourth century, and it has been used in very sophisticated ways by men like Leonard Hodgson in this century. Augustine used the psychological analogy in the fifth century, and it has been used recently by Claude Welch and others.

Each analogy is always in danger of falling into error. The psychological analogy has difficulty accounting for the threeness of God and so it always faces the danger of Sabellianism or modalism. This heresy, condemned in the third century, taught that the Father, Son, and Spirit were temporary revelations of a unipersonal God. God is not really Father, Son, and Spirit. It is just that he relates to men in these three ways at different times.

The social analogy also leans toward a heresy, that of tri-theism. When God is likened to three human beings it sounds very much like there are three gods. The problem for the theologian who uses this analogy is to try to express an understanding of the unity of God that will maintain monotheism.

How can one decide which of these two analogies to employ when speaking of God? I believe that, while in a limited sense we may employ both (using each to illustrate one point), still we must finally come down on one side or the other. Which shall it be?

For me, the answer lies in asking what it is that has been revealed to us. Has God shown us more clearly his Oneness or his Threeness? If what is clear to us is his unity, then we must use the one-person analogy (psychological analogy) and attempt to understand the mystery of his threeness. If he has shown his threeness more clearly, then we must use the three-person analogy (social analogy) and attempt to understand the mystery of his unity. What has he shown us?

We usually assume that it is his unity that is most clearly revealed. But while it is clearly revealed that there is only one God (against polytheism), the nature of that unity is not clearly revealed. But the nature of God's threeness is clearly revealed. So I believe that we know what his threeness is like (three persons); our difficulty is to try to understand the unity of the three.

The real strength of the social analogy is that it accounts for the facts of Jesus and the Spirit. It "fits" the picture of Jesus praying to the Father and sending the Spirit. It fits the picture of the Spirit come from the Father and testifying of the Son.

Therefore I elect to use the social analogy. How, then, can tri-theism be avoided? How are we to understand the unity of God?

The only theologian known to me who has recently attempted to examine closely the unity of God is Leonard Hodgson. He pointed out that we should not be surprised if the unity of God puzzles us, since after all, our own unity is a mystery. What is it that unites the various activities, ideas, emotions, values of a man? What unites the various relationships in which a man stands? It is not simplicity or the absence of multiplicity. It is a unifying power or force that binds together all our experiences into one life. Similarly God is not characterized by the absence of multiplicity. Rather the Father, Son, and Spirit are united by a great force which make their life one life. Augustine long ago said that it is love which binds together the Three Persons into one. I expect that is very near the truth. God the Father, Son, and Spirit is the one living God because he lives one life, a life of eternal love.

A Practical Implication

Those of us who are not Jews would never have known the God of Abraham except through his Son Jesus. And Jesus would have remained for us one more person in the past except for the ongoing experience of "life in Christ" which is a product of the Spirit's work in the church. So we who have salvation and are practicing Christian living are trinitarian in our practice, just as the early church was.

It is not good for our experience to differ from our understanding. We should try to understand what our experience is telling us. Perhaps it is time we became trinitarian in our thinking about God, that is, in our theology. Then practice and faith can join together in the worship and service of the one true God, Father, Son, and Holy Spirit.

For further reading:

The best short statement is surely Leonard Hodgson's *How Can God be Both One and Three?*, to which I referred above. For the alternative view see Claude Welch, *In This Name*. A helpful history is the article by H.E.W. Turner entitled "Doctrine of the Trinity" in Alan Richardson, ed., *A Dictionary of Christian Theology*.

INDEXES

INDEX OF NAMES

INDEX OF SUBJECTS